CARE
PACKAGE

ALSO BY SYLVESTER McNUTT III

<u>Books</u>

The Accelerated: Success Is a Choice

The Dear Queen Journey: A Path to Self-Love

Dear Soul: Love after Pain

*Dear Love Life: Efficient Dating
in The Technology Era*

This Is What Real Love Feels Like

Lust for Life

*Free Your Energy: The Path to Freedom,
Mental Clarity, and a Life of Enjoyment*

Loving Yourself Properly

CARE PACKAGE

Harnessing the Power of Self-Compassion to Heal & Thrive

SYLVESTER McNUTT III

HAY HOUSE

Carlsbad, California • New York City
London • Sydney • New Delhi

Published in the United Kingdom by:
Hay House UK Ltd, The Sixth Floor, Watson House,
54 Baker Street, London W1U 7BU
Tel: +44 (0)20 3927 7290; Fax: +44 (0)20 3927 7291; www.hayhouse.co.uk

Published in the United States of America by:
Hay House Inc., PO Box 5100, Carlsbad, CA 92018-5100
Tel: (1) 760 431 7695 or (800) 654 5126
Fax: (1) 760 431 6948 or (800) 650 5115; www.hayhouse.com

Published in Australia by:
Hay House Australia Ltd, 18/36 Ralph St, Alexandria NSW 2015
Tel: (61) 2 9669 4299; Fax: (61) 2 9669 4144; www.hayhouse.com.au

Published in India by:
Hay House Publishers India, Muskaan Complex, Plot No.3, B-2,
Vasant Kunj, New Delhi 110 070
Tel: (91) 11 4176 1620; Fax: (91) 11 4176 1630; www.hayhouse.co.in

A catalogue record for this book is available from the British Library.

Tradepaper ISBN: 978-1-83782-193-8
E-book ISBN: 978-1-4019-7664-4
Audiobook ISBN: 978-1-4019-7665-1

This book was previously published with ISBN: 978-0-6921-1155-0
Printed and bound by CPI Group (UK) Ltd, Croydon, CR0 4YY

*I dedicate this book to those people
who are looking for a ray of light.
I hope and pray that you find healing,
fun, and direction.
I'm rooting for you.*

CONTENTS

FOREWORD

Healing is really hard, and yet healing changes everything. As a grief and trauma therapist in private practice in New York City, I see a lot of unhappiness, disconnect, trauma, conflict, and helplessness. I've also endured my own fair share of loss and heartache along the way. Healing work can be a godsend—a path that can bring true, lasting healing and new ways of seeing yourself and your life—and I'm a believer in not "skirting the work" with quick fixes, emotional Band-Aids, or spiritual bypassing often seen in the wellness industry. That said, sometimes in healing there is this thing called "the gradual instant," when you're chugging along the path and all of a sudden something really hits you and things begin to make sense; you have an insight you worked and longed for, in one lightning-speed moment. That's what this book brought to me when I first read it. A gut punch of matter-of-fact insight—a swift lightning bolt of truth I needed to both see and share.

In my therapy work, I emphasize truth-seeking in the process; so when healing comes, we know it's genuine. That often means looking at the hard stuff—our blind spots—those behaviors and patterns we often would rather overlook or ignore, or simply parts of ourselves we just haven't gotten to know. I get it, who wants to get to know and take ownership of the "ugly or destructive" parts? And yet, if we don't look at the whole picture of our lives, we rarely will find *lasting* healing, because we are only looking to heal what other people have given to us, as opposed to healing the whole wound. Though that can sound daunting, it doesn't mean healing needs to be endless and relentlessly overwhelming. Sometimes, it can come in shorter bursts of aha moments and gentle realizations.

When I first came across the intuitive, inspiring, down-to-earth but spectacularly motivating human vortex that is Sylvester McNutt III, it was through this book. It came into my life when I needed someone to just tell it like it is to my heart—to give it to me straight, so to speak. And, this is coming from a person who finds matters of the heart her specialty and waxes poetic about emotions every day. I firmly believe the power of the books we choose has to do with timing. What's happening in our lives when we pick up a certain book? Are we feeling like a victim to our circumstances? Are we stuck in a cycle we haven't been able to find our way out of yet? Are we really in the dark abyss of our struggle or have we climbed out and are looking back on the struggle? This book speaks directly to all of it. Sylvester helps to elicit our truths and the aspects of our challenges that we can control but also empowers and uplifts like the absolute perfect cup of coffee. There are times we need tender revelations and there are times we need hard truths to help shift our mindset. Luckily, you can find both here.

It can feel so hard to see, recognize, or accept the light ahead when we have been in the darkness for so long. It can feel nearly impossible to see another way, another perspective, or to hold on to the fragile thread of hope when life has handed us challenge after challenge, years of struggle, endless losses, and the fear that it may never get better.

Yet, Sylvester seems to speak straight to the weary heart. When I first read this book, I remember feeling like he was looking straight into my eyes, telling me to look another way, to see something different when it came to a repetitive thought I'd had after learning of my mother's end-stage cancer diagnosis. It was a game changer for me, as someone prone to overthinking and analyzing (pitfalls of the trade, I suppose!). The insight Sylvester gave to me in these pages wasn't about running away or emotionally bypassing what I couldn't fix. It was about embracing what was in front of me and taking a single step in my power at a time. It was a refreshing change from the therapeutic insight I was so used to hearing and reading, and something I have since adopted in my own work: getting to the heart of the matter and doing the next best thing.

Since I read this book, I've had the good fortune of becoming colleagues and friends with Sylvester, thanks to the publishing world. I can tell you this: the insight in the pages is a true reflection of the remarkable, honest, steadfast, and contagiously galvanizing human he is in real life. So when I was asked to write this foreword, I was deeply honored. To get to be here with you as you pick up this book and decide if it's the right one for you is a privilege and gift.

Genuine healing work can be scary, painful, exhausting, confusing, and at times, really overwhelming. I sit with people every day in my therapy practice who show up, despite all of that, because freedom, peace, contentment, and authentic, healthy connections have become more important than remaining in the painful patterns; conflict-ridden relationships; suffocating, dismissive, or agonizing family dynamics; undervaluing careers; or self-destructive ways of being in life. I respect the courage it takes to make a change more than I can say, and being a traveling companion with those brave souls is an honor for me on a daily basis. But, even then, I know that sometimes we need more. We need the books and the music and the podcasts and the memes. We need the articles and the social media communities, too. Healing can take a modern village these days, and so, I invite you to consider this book a part of your village, just as I have.

Living life with a focus on embracing what's in front of us and honestly, courageously befriending and engaging with it, doesn't have to be a lofty mental health ideal set aside for the elite. It can and should be a way of life for everyone. Healing, showing up, staying consistent, telling the truth, seeking connection, and moving toward a healthy life and lifestyle is the goal; and the map to support you in navigating through is what is offered here.

In the pages ahead, you will find that Sylvester speaks from experience, but also with a bird's-eye view that can help us all to get out of the weeds of our self-destructive dynamics and see a broader, healthier way to move forward. That's no easy feat for anyone. The themes in this book cover the pain of the human condition with honesty and care, but also with steadfast motivation to keep going, even when the path feels too hard.

I keep this book by my bedside for the moments I need a "care package" at the end of a long, harrowing day, as it has given me those beautiful bursts of comfort that remind me I can try again tomorrow.

My wish for you is that you feel what I did when reading this book: seen, validated, cared for, motivated, inspired, and moved to both look at and do things differently. I wish you a new perspective that puts your heart and well-being at the forefront of your life. I wish you a renewed sense of self that reminds you of how freaking strong, capable, lovable, and worthy you are, because, well, no matter what you think or what you have been through, that's the truth. Above all, I hope you feel what's at the heart of this book: caring, camaraderie, and the sense that you do not have to struggle alone. We got this.

With sincere care and gratitude,
Gina
Gina Moffa, LCSW
Psychotherapist and author of *Moving On Doesn't Mean Letting Go: A Modern Guide to Navigating Loss*

INTRODUCTION

A Vulnerable Note to You

This is my most vulnerable book. I believe that I am a happy and healthy person; however, we all have many different layers. We are all just like a fresh onion. My attempt here is to peel back some of the layers that are stopping me from moving forward. I have a few obstacles to overcome. Will I do it? I don't know how long it will take, but I have to at least try. I believe you are reading this because we have a similar goal: to truly heal from pain. And that's the beautiful part of this journey—the part where we admit that we have been through a lot and finally open ourselves up to face our demons. If you've read any of my books before, you may think that I'm always vulnerable, but I promise you that *Care Package* offers a level of vulnerability that I have never reached in any of my other books. I dive into scars, I dive into self, and the introspection and self-reflection here are scary. My purpose for exposing myself is to first heal me and then to offer you relatable words or stories that may help heal you.

I love you. I say that for two reasons. One: getting my words out into the marketplace was a very long and hard process. I lost friendships and jobs over this. I lost my sanity and my former self, and I have given up everything to do this. I am forever grateful for people like you, because without you, I wouldn't be here doing this. As artists, as humans, sometimes we lose sight of what matters most, and that's the people you touch, in my humble opinion. That's the first reason I love you. The second reason I love you is because you're willing to invest in yourself. I'm a big believer in investing in yourself because it makes your life better and it makes the worlds better. You're willing to take risks to expand, to heal, to grow your mind, or to see things that are completely opposite of you in order to help you reach your potential. If that's not real love, then I don't know what love is. Now let's talk about the structure of *Care Package*.

I like to write introspectively first and then to you second. The reason for this is because I don't want my text to come off as if I'm taking the role of authority. Oftentimes we look at gurus, writers, preachers, teachers, helpers, and others in positions of power as the be-all and end-all.

I never want you to do that with me or my work. I don't consider myself to be any of those things listed above. In my mind, I am simply an artist. We are two students on a journey together, looking for truth, and I want my writing to look within for me and for you. I do not have answers. This book is not about answers. *Care Package* will not save you. It will not change you, for it is not the power—you are the power. The sole purpose of my words is to shine light on something that is inside of you, to ask you questions, to cause conflict with how you think, to offer words that show a path to finding what you need at that moment.

Nothing that I say is truth, valid, or important. I am only a messenger. You are the power, you are the guru, and you are the one.

The excerpts, shorter poems, and lists help me connect to my readers who cannot afford my books. I post those for them—for the kid who has no money but uses Twitter to find hope. I post the small excerpt for the woman who struggles to find the strength to keep going. For the man who is on the verge of breaking down, I want him to find my words, and I want him to know that it will be okay. I post my words on the Internet so we can look back and find the words that we need to maintain our lives, stay inspired, and heal as deeply as possible.

I love the art of writing, creating, and sharing thought. This is my seventh book, and I cannot explain to you how humbled I am that people keep reading my work. I will never take it for granted. I wake up every day and focus on expanding my mind, my perspective, and my understanding of the world. I am humbled greatly that people like you spend your hard-earned money to view my content. I will never take your effort for granted, because you spent your hard-earned money on my words, and that inspires me to go as deep as I can, to be as real as I can, and to never be perfect but to be what I am. Thank you for embracing this project. I love you; I appreciate you. I am humbled by you, and I hope we can continue to build our friendship through words. You give my words meaning; you give my words power.

I believe *Care Package* tackles some of the tough issues that prevent us from moving forward—some rooted in childhood, some that occurred during the teen years, and almost all plaguing some, if not all, adults. I believe the outline of this book is perfect for healing. There are two main sections: Tending To The Wounds and Treating Yourself With Love and Compassion. We start off talking about alignment and recognizing that we are off. We shift to walking away from pain and letting go, and then we learn how to set boundaries. The middle of the book focuses on guilt and codependency, which leads us to self-care and putting yourself first. The last few chapters round us out and give us new flesh: overcoming anxiety, living in the moment, continuing to love, and finally healing.

You'll notice that each section can be taught as a curriculum or as a healing process. I created *Care Package* so that one day it can be taught in schools or to people who want true healing. I believe these are topics that we don't talk about enough in our society. *Care Package* is my effort to be the change I want to see in the world.

PART I

TENDING TO THE WOUNDS

ONE

ALIGNMENT

I find it madly ironic that when one thing is out of alignment, an entire project can go wrong. If the NASA engineers are off by one inch, it will result in a fatal catastrophe. If the trajectory of your jump shot is not optimal, you will shoot at a lower rate.

If you have the wrong friends, you will produce the wrong results. My friends, alignment is everything. In order to fix anything in business, in sports, in relationship matters, or within, we must always start with the observation of alignment. Alignment helps us figure out what pieces of the puzzle are in the wrong places, so let's start there.

HOW TO IDENTIFY WHEN YOU
ARE OUT OF ALIGNMENT

I have dealt with back pain for the last two years. Something is not right in my midback area. I played football for 10+ years. I lift weights and play basketball three times a week.

If you know just a little bit about the human body, you know that these activities cause stress on the body. As far as I understand, stress on the body isn't always a bad thing. If you want to grow your muscles, working out adds a stress that seems to give positive results—stronger muscles. However, not all stress is good, especially if said stress causes pain; then it is definitely not good.

The pain that I have in my midback causes me a great deal of unbearable stress. I experience restless nights of tossing and turning, and it slows down my day-to-day functionality. It's hidden pain because I never talk about it with friends and family members; plus, you cannot see it since I do not limp. I am very strong physically and mentally, so people who are simply observing me are unable to identify this pain that I deal with. And that's the thing about pain. Sometimes it's on our face as tears, and other times it's hidden deep within. People on the outside have no idea what we're fighting. The only people who know I have back trouble are the doctors whom I've seen. I'm not ashamed of the pain. I just didn't care to openly talk about it until this moment, because it seemed irrelevant. I woke up the other day and could barely move. My neck was tight, my back was throbbing in pain, and my shoulders felt like I had lifted a truck the day before.

I could barely put on a shirt. Instead of feeling sorry for myself and cornering myself into the victim role, where we typically all love to go when we feel pain, I decided to make a plan that would help me abolish the back pain and ultimately give me the proper back *alignment*. The back pain is helping me understand the rest of the world in a way that I have never seen it. It's poetic. Can you see that?

Because of my back pain, my life is not operating on the highest vibration possible. When I use the word *vibration*, I am referring to the energetic volume or potency of something. For example, the sound of your mom humming to you as a kid is a high vibration—one that soothed you, made you go to sleep, or feel safe. The feeling you get when you are at a gas station at night is a low vibration—one of fear or alertness.

I'm dealing with pain every single day, and it's seeping in so deep that it's affecting other activities, like rest, the ability to relax, and my inner peace. I want to heal this aspect of my life.

You can look at your life right now and observe something that is out of alignment: your job, your mental health—hell, maybe you have back pain too, or you have a best friend who is crossing borders and boundaries. No matter what, we all have something in our lives that is simply not aligned the way it could be. Typically, it's something like back pain, something that you don't truly feel like explaining or expressing to everyone.

So I challenge you to do as I've done for myself: name it. A therapist may tell you something like, "name it to claim it," which essentially means you have to be real and authentic when identifying what your pain point is and take ownership over your healing process. Become fully aware of what is limiting or restricting you, without putting yourself down. Is it my fault that I have this back pain? Yes, I chose to play a contact sport. Do I deserve to beat myself up over it? Absolutely not. Do I deserve to be free of the pain? Yes, I do. I want you to understand that most of us add pain on top of pain, and that will never ever solve the problem of pain.

If you want to rid yourself of pain, you have to release the pain bodies, the triggers, or the actual entity that is causing you the burden. For the sake of consistency, I am going to stick to my back-pain analogy, because not only is it true but it's also easy to understand and transfer over into your life. It's something that I hope you can take with you and remember as you go through life. I want you to think, *Damn, is my back out of alignment like 2017 Sylvester, or is it aligned like 2018 Sylvester?*

As December 2017 started and I committed to ridding myself of this damn back pain, the first step I took after identifying the pain was to look at what I was doing and what I had already done around this problem. That is step two as far as aligning yourself goes. If you are just getting started on your own healing journey, these landmarks serve as a great opening act for the process. Keep these in mind:

1. Commit to the process of healing.

2. "Name it to claim it" to take ownership of your healing.

3. Take inventory of what you have done.

4. See what information is available for you.

5. Find out what options and actions are available to progress.

WHAT BEHAVIORS AM I DOING RIGHT NOW, AND WHAT DO I NEED TO CHANGE?

Most people are unwilling to change. Most people are so stuck in their ways that they'll stop at this first step. I can't sugarcoat this enough. If you are serious about transforming your life, you have to be completely committed to change. Change is hard, and identifying that you are the one messing up your life—not The Man, not society, not your husband or wife, but you—is a responsibility that most humans never want to bear. Here's the crazy thing about accepting that you and only you have messed up: it gives you power. And yes, in some situations we were unlucky, we were the victim, we were at the wrong place at the wrong time. In that case, I want to make sure you understand that your time and energy is valuable. I want you to focus on healing and on what you can do to change this path. It's tough, especially if there is an injustice or an abuse of power. Yes, it pisses me off too, but we have to take our power back. We do that by healing.

The fact is that you and only you can fix it. It's understanding and accepting that you have always had the power deep inside of you, but because of your thoughts, you have never empowered yourself enough to feel like you have the power. The next step toward aligning yourself correctly is to make a new plan. The best way to make a plan is to layer it. You want to have short-range, midrange, and long-range goals inside of the plan. Allow yourself space to adjust the plan as you go. Having a rigid plan forces you to remain one way, when the pain itself is there to help you grow. Sometimes we outgrow plans and the pace of the plan, and the only way to ensure that you do not trap yourself is to remain completely fluid and agile throughout the plan. The final step toward fixing the alignment is to listen to your body and your mind and to observe how your life changes after you start executing the plan.

Back to my back. You already know that I am dealing with an immense amount of pain, so the next question is, What did I do, or what am I doing, to rid myself of it? Following the steps that I just gave you, the first thing I did was realize that I needed to sleep more. I realized that I needed to play basketball at least one day less per week because the stress on my joints is no longer beneficial to me. I have decided that I am committing to acupuncture and cupping for the remainder of the year while also adding two yoga sessions per week. I've done yoga before, and I've done acupuncture. I am aware of the healing properties of both, but what I needed was a commitment to it as well as the subtraction of something that I enjoy. Right now three days a week of full-court basketball could be having a negative impact. Many people are not willing to stop doing what they've been doing even though they are the ones who claim they want to change. Funny how that works out. I made my commitment to a new plan, one that feels like it will give me new results, and if it doesn't work, that's okay—at least I was willing to try something different.

When you feel like you are out of alignment, that is your body, your mind, your heart, and your intuition telling you that you must adjust. Do not be the type of person who ignores the inner dialogue. That's like punching yourself in the face during winter while you're walking blindfolded down a one-way street. If you ignore yourself, you will have an accident, and it won't be pretty. On the next page, I've listed these steps for people who enjoy numbers and bullet points.

Four Ways to Realign Your Life

1. Identify the problem.

2. Become fully aware of what you've done to cause it and what you're doing to fix it.

3. Make a new, flexible plan to attack the problem.

4. Listen to yourself and observe your life changing as you execute the plan.

Sometimes pain is on our face
as tears, and other times it's
hidden deep within, and people
on the outside have no idea what
we're fighting.

— s. mcnutt

You are strong enough
and wise enough to get
through this current struggle.
The divine wisdom is already
inside. Speak in a powerful
way about what you can do,
lean into the help, and
never give up on your
evolution. You are ready!

— s. mcnutt

Your ability to align your life correctly is not determined by other people. If you want it, you will find a way.

If you want it, you will stay late or show up early.

If you want it, you will release any excuses.

You will live in alignment with what you want.

You will be consistent and patient as you show up for the life you want to create.

— s. mcnutt

Life will give you a hundred reasons to cry, but the fact that you still have a heartbeat is your thousand reasons to smile and laugh.

— s. mcnutt

When things go wrong in your life, you have to focus on getting stronger. Getting stronger doesn't mean acting like you have it all together. Strength is also allowing certain things to fall apart.

— s. mcnutt

When negative energy finds you, never fight back. If you do, you become it. Develop boundaries with that energy. And if you can't, learn to walk away and choose peace over war.

— s. mcnutt

The people you knew will start to feel like strangers if they do not grow with you. It's okay to love from afar as you grow apart. It's okay to appreciate and value them as changes occur.

— s. mcnutt

Put yourself in a situation that
makes you happy.

— s. mcnutt

Never be rigid. The wind
flows; it moves around objects
no matter what; be able to
flow like the wind.

— s. mcnutt

If you have to break a
commitment to keep your life
aligned, do it. Things change.
People change. Situations change.
I believe in commitment and
working through things, but
some commitments don't need
to be kept. Learning to honor
when something needs to end
will free you.

— s. mcnutt

Nowadays, we want
things to happen so
fast. Slow down;
trust the process.

— s. mcnutt

If a train goes too fast, it could
easily derail. Don't assume
you need to give up when you
run into problems. Sometimes
you're just going too fast, or you
want it to happen too quickly.
Slow down. Allow things to
play out slower, without force,
without control.

— s. mcnutt

Fact: obsessive overthinking
never helps you. Let it be what it
will be. Let it flow naturally.

— s. mcnutt

You're always at work. Make
sure the job aligns with your
core values. Pick a career
that supports your soul. Do
something that brings you alive
or gives you mental challenges.
We spend a lot of time in our
vocation; let's make sure it
delivers us multiple rewards.

— s. mcnutt

THREE TIPS THAT WILL HELP YOU
ALIGN WITH THE RIGHT JOB

All across the world, we tell our friends the same thing: do something you love. You know what's funny about that? It's always people who do not do what they love who are telling other people to do what they love. I'm not going to give you that cookie-cutter advice, for three reasons: One, that's not useful information. Two, you might not know what you love, and three, you might be doing what needs to be done for survival, and I'm never going to judge you for that. These three tips will help you pick the right job when the time is right.

1. **Commit to curiosity.** It's amazing to me how we expect 18-year-old kids to know their majors for college, what their lives will be, and to be set on this "plan." I know people in their thirties and forties who have no clue what they're doing, yet we expect kids to know, and that expectation is foolish. The best thing I did with my life was attempt a bunch of different things until I figured out what I liked, regardless of age. Don't think this is limited to just jobs either. You should be trying different activities, foods, and different people too. *Disclaimer*: If you jump from job to job every four to six months, it will look like you do not understand commitment, and this could hinder the hiring process. Be very methodical in your approach to leaving jobs.

2. **Get what you're worth.** This is a paradox because there are times you have to go through a situation that actually helps you get what you're worth, and other times you have to stay to a point where you realize, *Damn, I'm*

not getting treated the way I deserve. You must always have an open mind. Knowing your worth is about knowing what you can contribute and also knowing what you're not willing to take or settle for.

I left a really "good" job because I didn't feel like I was getting what I was worth. Most people are unwilling to quit a $60,000–$70,000 per-year job. I knew I was worth more than that. I knew I could make that amount in a month. I knew I could double or triple that yearly salary, but I also knew that I needed the job to help me build it. I stayed at my job and built my business on the side. Most people are unwilling to do that much work. Most people claim they're worth more, but they are lazy and unfocused. If you feel like you deserve more, there are two things that you must have at all times to create the success you want: *vision* and *drive*. In the example I gave you, keep in mind that maximizing my income was a priority, and it was directly connected to my "worth."

3. Embrace the duality of choosing. There is no right or wrong way to look at this. It is always about listening to your heart and making the best decisions possible for your situation. There is value in taking a lower-paying job if it will bring you happiness; however, there is value in giving yourself more security with the higher-paying job. Looking for higher pay or looking for what you love may not be what's best for you. You may have to combine the two. This is where a lot of people get lost. They don't know if they should do what they love or if they should secure the bag. I am a person who does what he loves for a living, which is to create content daily, write my books, create videos, and do public speaking. This type of job also supports my wealth and wellness, and that was important to me. One of the most important things we can do is choose a vocation that is in alignment with who we are and what we aim to give. And if you don't know fully, that is okay. Invest in learning, in education, in experience, and give yourself a chance to find *what you love*. In my specific situation, I always knew what I wanted to do. I just didn't know how I was going to create it as a job, so at first I just did it for free so I could get better. I did it for free until people decided to pay me for products, services, ideas, and my time, and then I had to figure out how to multiply it so it could be consistent. Finding the right job, the dream job, takes time. You have to grow and acquire enough skills and talent to execute the job you seek. It's a process, not a light switch, so you have to be patient with the process and trust that each season has a greater purpose for you.

Suspend ego; pause, observe the energy around you, understand, and listen more than you speak.

— s. mcnutt

There is value in taking a lower-paying job if it will bring a higher amount of happiness.

— s. mcnutt

I wish I could make
everyone understand
how important this
statement is: *go where
you are wanted*.

— s. mcnutt

The right friends will
challenge you to do better.
They'll see greatness inside
of you before you do.

— s. mcnutt

THREE IMPORTANT TOOLS THAT WILL HELP YOU ALIGN WITH THE RIGHT PEOPLE

1. Become fully aware of their goals, their ambitions, and the actions they're currently taking to manifest the life that they claim they want. They always say that your life is similar to the five people you interact with most, and if that is true for you, it is important that your friends somewhat align with your goals and ambitions. Of course, respect that everyone is on their own path and time line, but this still matters.

2. Ask them probing questions about how they feel about pain and love, and what success looks like to them. Aligning yourself with the right friends will save you from pain and can introduce you to love or success.

3. Figure out quickly if they're the type of people who will be honest with you. Why? Because you need people whom you can trust, who can give you an honest perception of how you behave. Honest friends help sharpen you, they help inspire you, they help you see yourself without your ego.

Break up with the friends who
are full of ego and pride, friends
who claim to do no wrong.

— s. mcnutt

I no longer chase anything
or anyone. I work for what I
want and remain patient while
going after it.

— s. mcnutt

CHARACTERISTICS OF
FRIENDSHIPS IN ALIGNMENT

- Challenge you to grow
- Listen to your shortcomings
- Provide realistic feedback about your skill sets and abilities
- Fulfill hierarchal need for human connection
- Learn and share personal interests
- Have dialogue about intimate relationships to gain perspective or confirmation
- Engage in mostly fun and enjoyable environments
- Provide support mentally or emotionally through diverse life moments

TWO

WALKING AWAY FROM PAIN

There are too many adults walking around with pain that has never been talked about. We mask it, we hide it, we keep it in the closet because we are afraid to wear the outfits of pain.

This time in my life is dedicated
to healing deeply, while
attracting happiness.

— s. mcnutt

Be completely aware of your
pain, but don't allow it to define
who you are. Pain is an emotion
that passes.

— s. mcnutt

In 2014 my father passed away. He was young, only 51 at the time. In my opinion, that is way too early to die. I talked in detail about the way he raised me and how it gave me pain and trauma, and I don't write these words in vain or to throw shade on someone's legacy. I respect every single person I write about. I am very grateful for my experiences with him and my mother, two people who caused me a great deal of pain. But like I told you in the last chapter, *they did the best they could with what they had, and they tried their best to provide love.* And that is why I choose to forgive them. My father and I did not speak for about five years during my college days, but let me tell you the story of why. One summer I was attempting to leave the kitchen, and he demanded that I wash the dishes. I didn't feel like I needed to because they weren't my dishes. They were the dishes from him and his girlfriend, and I didn't feel like I should be responsible for their mess, because I wasn't there to create it. I was working full time at the Home Depot in Palatine, Illinois. I trained at my high school gym when I wasn't at work since it was across the street. I read books in my spare time, and, of course, I played some PlayStation because I was, and still am, a video game nerd.

At the time I felt like my life was very simple and organized. I was finally stepping out into my own realm of finding myself, as they say. I told him that I didn't feel like I was responsible for the dishes because I wasn't home. It wasn't my mess, and I didn't feel like I should be given busywork just because I was the child. I was 19 years old. Of course, anyone who is a parent may feel some entitlement, and you may align with my father. I understand. In this moment, his ego ran him, and he attacked me with a frying pan, demanding that I wash the dishes. Of course,

I defended myself, and he said that if I didn't wash the dishes, I had to leave the house immediately.

What do you think I did? I did exactly what you think I would do, exactly what I preach. I packed my bag and left because I realized my worth. I realized that regardless of our relationship, nobody had the right to treat me like that, attack me, or threaten me physically. No human being deserves to fight me, hurt me, or cause me bodily harm. I realized in that moment that nothing could destroy me, because I chose myself over this fake sense of security. I chose myself over family, over what was called love, but that wasn't love. It was one of the first moments in my life where I took control and power away from other people. It was scary, and it was not easy, but I had to choose my own happiness over everything.

That was a fucked-up moment in time, and again, I am still not mad at my father, because he did the best he could with what he had. His life was going down step-by-step, and just like a ship out to sea with a small hole in it, eventually the water will fill the vessel. If you do not patch the holes, eventually you will sink. *My father put me out.* That is one way you can look at it, and when I was that age I played the victim role, for sure. I told the story like he put me out. But now, with this consciousness that I have, I know the truth, and the truth is that *I put myself out.*

I didn't want my ship to sink like my father's. I didn't want to be unhappy like he was at the time. He had pain bodies inside of him that he never managed, and his behavior proved it. His behavior looked for other pain bodies, and even though I usually met him in that space, on this day I decided that those pain bodies would no longer have permission to participate in my experience called life.

SO WHAT HAPPENED NEXT?

This was the first time I was homeless. I wasn't sure what to do, actually. I had no plan, no savings. I had just gotten my first cell phone. I didn't have a car. I was filled with anger and rage because I thought to myself, *What type of parent puts his kid out on the street?* I went to the high school that I attended, and I sat outside. It was the summertime, and nobody was there. I went to this familiar place, and I took in several breaths. I surveyed the land, and for the first time in my life I felt free. This moment of chaos for other people brought me calm and peace. It brought me understanding and serenity. This moment of being homeless and formless brought a smile to my face. I remember saying to myself, *What am I going to do now?* I didn't obsess about going back. I didn't care to apologize, because I genuinely didn't feel like I had done anything wrong. I didn't care to backtrack at all. I only wanted to move forward. I feel like a lot of people go wrong when chaos happens in their lives, because they're rigid. They obsess about going backward, forcing what is broken, and it never works. I embrace the chaos. I believe in staying fluid and adaptable. I never try to change what is happening. I accept reality, and I use my skills to adapt.

Eventually, I got ahold of one of my teammates who found out that I was in this situation. His parents agreed to let me stay with them for the summer. I was very grateful for their hospitality and gratitude. They never asked me for anything other than to respect their house rules, and, of course, I did everything that was asked of me.

So let's conclude this here. To be completely vulnerable and honest, this situation brought me a lot of pain. It made me resent and hate my father. It made me develop a survivor's mindset. I developed a certain level of self-reliability because I never wanted to be in a situation like that again. This moment in my life caused me to truly care about making money, to learn how systems like renting an apartment or buying a house worked, and to figure out how to network with people. This very bad situation brought me so many great tools and some unruly inner emotions. I held on to the pain for years. I hated my father and chose not to speak to him for at least five years.

This next part is very important for your life. By not talking to him, what I thought I was doing was separating myself from pain, and I was. To me he was a representation of pain. I feared him. I feared dealing with him because he brought emotions out of me that made me uncomfortable. What I didn't know at the time was how deep my pain bodies were. I didn't know at that time that I was holding on to anger, resentment, fear, disdain, and a victim mindset. And one day someone said this to me: "Sylvester, your father is not going to be around forever. You need to forgive him for what he did to you, and you need to move on."

To this day I cannot remember who said it. In fact, it's either one of two people, or both of them, who said it. It was either my girlfriend at the time or my auntie Syl, short for Sylvia. I was open to receiving the message. I had matured because for the five years during that time whenever his name came up, it triggered me. Whenever someone talked about our relationship, I shut down and refused to talk. Again, this is how pain makes you act, especially when you decide that you don't want to deal with it. Finally, I decided that I was going to call him, and he answered. I told him how he made me feel, how he hurt me, and most importantly, I set a boundary. I set a boundary for how

I would be treated moving forward. I told him that if he couldn't meet me in this new space with new behaviors, then this would be the first and last conversation with me as a young adult. I was only 23 when we had this conversation. We stopped talking when I was 19. He reduced the ego that he had five years earlier, and he apologized. He accepted that he could've handled things differently, and he was open to starting a new relationship with me. I know for a fact that he was dealing with guilt and shame, and he felt like he had abused me. Although he never said it, I could feel the shame that he was dealing with, just like he could feel the anger that I was dealing with. That phone conversation gave us healing.

We were both able to let go of the past, and this allowed us to move forward. In my situation, I was fortunate to have what I call a *closure conversation*. However, I do have a very important asterisk. Do not—I repeat, do not—read what I just said and think that is your signal to call someone who abused you, who beat you, who caused you bodily harm. Do not. In fact, if it was that serious, it's best that you stay away. I feel fortunate that I had a forgiving person who was willing to change. I also developed an unreal level of strength through my weight training and mental strength through my spiritual awakening. I no longer felt like he, or anyone for that matter, could harm me, and that is part of why I decided to rekindle our relationship. I know my fans take my words very literally, and I hope you see that I am simply telling you a story about my life—about what I went through, about how I felt, about what I decided to do. If I didn't feel safe, I wouldn't contact a person no matter what. If I felt like that person was still violent, I wouldn't deal with him or her at all. That's just me. I hope you do not misinterpret my words. This is very important.

LOCKING PAIN INTO YOUR MIND

We suffer greatly because we don't understand our minds, the words we use, or how we associate with and deal with pain. The first step toward healing from pain is to become completely aware of how you choose to associate with pain. Look at the differences between these two sets of statements:

> "I went through a lot when I was younger."
> "Nobody cared about me when I was younger."

> or

> "Why does this always happen to me?"
> "What can I learn about this situation?"

Simply altering and manipulating the words you use can literally change how your mind associates with pain. I don't care to identify with my past pain, but I also don't think it's healthy to dismiss it and act like it never occurred. I'll give you an example to illustrate what I am saying here. My father and mother had no issue with spankings and whippings as a way to discipline me and my siblings. Personally, I never felt like it did anything other than instill hate and fear inside me. As a result, I was a child who didn't feel loved, didn't feel like I could speak my mind, and never cared to have dialogue with anyone, because I was conditioned to think that people would hurt me if they didn't like what I said or if my behavior didn't align with what they wanted. Of course, I had to heal from and unlearn that pain, but for a while I suffered because I chose to identify with the pain. I didn't accept what I told you earlier: *healing is a choice*. Now that I know healing is a choice, I can heal from the childhood pain and conditioning that my mind has identified with. You're going to ask me how I healed from the childhood trauma, so let's go deeper.

Process to Heal from Childhood Pain

1. Stop identifying with the pain. The pain is in the past. It is something that happened; it is not something that is happening.

2. Realize that you have to forgive the people who caused you the pain, even if you don't want to.

3. Learn the psychology about how your childhood traumas have affected you as an adult (e.g., fear, abuse, and abandonment). Do the research to figure out the end results of such treatment so you can know how it affects you today. If the research is too hard, seek therapy and counseling to uncover those answers with a professional—it will help.

4. Learn that living in the present moment will always heal you. Living in the past forces you to align with it, especially if there is pain. Living in the future forces you to be anxious—live here.

FREEDOM FROM PAIN

Once you are able to fully see through your consciousness that you have been locking pain into your mind, then and only then will you unlock it. I gave you an example above about the type of language that haunts you and fixates you into the abyss of pain. Do you want to suffer, or do you want to be free? When you change those words to "What can I learn about this situation?" then the entire situation changes. You just placed yourself in the presence of power, in the presence of healing, and this why healing is a choice. You have the choice to change your words, which changes your outlook and, as a result, changes your life. I want to go a little bit deeper with locking pain into your mind. Paying attention to the words you use has the power to do one of do two things: *free you* or *enslave you*. Enslavement is the pain on the face of animals at the zoo. Freedom is when you watch sports and you watch the winning team win the championship. Which do you want? Which do you deserve? I know for a fact you're going to say that you want freedom from pain, but do you believe that? Do you genuinely, in the bottom of your heart, believe that you deserve that? Once you answer that question, a million pounds of pressure will be lifted from your soul.

PAIN IS A CYCLE UNTIL YOU BREAK IT

When I was a young boy, I was always getting into fights with other boys. This makes sense, considering that I was raised in a violent household and a violent environment. I became silent because it was normalized in that area. It was a cycle of pain—at lunch, after school, before school, with my brothers, and with my dad. With the childlike consciousness, I couldn't tell you why then, but I can now. There were pains that lived inside of me. Eckhart Tolle refers to them as pain bodies in his book *The Power of Now*[1]. When you have a pain body, it's like a heat-seeking missile that has been launched from a plane. Its sole mission is to search for pain—to find a host, a target that will help keep it alive. To search for pain inside of other people. To find people who will meet this pain and welcome it.

The reason you have toxic relationships over and over again is because you've never healed the pain, and the pain lives inside of you. As a result of never dealing with the pain, it attracts people who can continue the cycle of pain. That's why it was so easy for me to fight boys, to argue with teachers, and to talk crazy to my parents when I was younger—because the pain was given to me. And, of course, I was an innocent child, so I had no idea what was going on. I took the pain. I became a host for the pain. I accepted the pain and helped it grow because I searched for other pain bodies. So the questions I have to ask you are these: *How much longer can you continue to repeat these cycles of pain? When are you going to change the way your life is going?* And the most important question that you must have for yourself is this: *Is it possible that I can stop the cycles, starting with my behavior and my perspectives?*

In my experience, starting with these questions will be the foundation of resolution. Once I accepted that it was possible for me to change, that I deserved more, and that I did not want to suffer, that is when my life changed for the better. That is when I had a spiritual awakening. I realized that I did not need to fight anyone. I realized that I could have a peaceful life, and most importantly, I realized that I deserved it. It was my duty to deliver this to myself. Please take an inventory of your life. Look at the last six or seven years and just observe the interactions—the friendships, the dating partners—and become fully aware of the entire spectrum of how things went. Become aware of what you brought to the madness. Become aware of it all, but do not label or judge yourself. This exercise is not done because you need to place blame; it's done to increase awareness so you can rise and create a new life. That's it. Blame is not important to me. If you're going to blame anyone, blame yourself, because blaming yourself will give you the power to fix it. But for the purpose of this exercise, do not blame—just become aware. Over the next few pages, I'd like to address why you need to be aware of your pain without judging or blaming anyone for the pain and how being aware of your pain, in a way, may free you from it.

Healing from pain is a choice.
You have to consciously decide
that you deserve to feel free,
that you deserve to let go of the
weight that has been holding you
down for too long.

— s. mcnutt

Break up with the mindset
that you have haters—that
people are against you, that
you have enemies. Thinking
you have haters will manifest
low-vibrational energy. Instead,
think about true friendships
and genuine energy. That's how
you use the universe to attract
powerful allies.

— s. mcnutt

A truly aware person understands the power of thoughts and never has the "me against the world" mindset. Thinking people are against you will isolate you; it will hurt you more. Trust and know that there are good people who want to bring you positive energy.

— s. mcnutt

DESTROYING THE "ME AGAINST THE WORLD" MINDSET

My entire attitude switched for the better when I abolished the "me against the world" mindset. I grew up with the "me against the world" perspective because of my pain. I felt like everyone wanted to hurt me because people in the past had. I did what most adults do, which is carry the pain. Therapists refer to it as *survivor's mindset.* When you feel like you've been abandoned and left for dead, and nobody wants you, defeating the odds makes you a survivor; it makes you a warrior. When you've been abandoned emotionally, you develop strength within, but you also don't let people get close to you. You try your best to keep evil energy out, but a mask comes over you because you often judge other people wrongly or develop a victim mentality. Why do you develop these walls and become jaded? Because you feel like people will leave once you let them in, or they will come in just to hurt you. These thoughts are normal; we are just protecting ourselves. It's called self-preservation. I knew I needed to grow out of the extreme paranoia, and I did, and if you have that, you will too. Just be patient reading *Care Package* and be patient with yourself, and you'll slowly alleviate it.

That's what happened to me, and I knew I needed to grow out of the "me against the world" mindset. Later, in my twenties, I had a spiritual awakening after realizing that I needed to dedicate myself to healing, purpose, and a total integration of my experience. I realized that there's no such thing as an enemy or a hater. I knew I was healing and in alignment when I realized that I didn't have any enemies. Mind you, I grew up playing football and sports teaches you that there is always an enemy, a challenge, and opponent. I played in college, and I played arena football. I'm supercompetitive, but after my spiritual awakening, I realized that I do not have any opponents. I realized that the only opponent I'll ever have in life is my mind. When I have inner conflict, that causes me more pain than any other person is possible of causing. People are not bad. People are not out to get you. People genuinely don't go around trying to hurt others. Let's not be naïve. Of course there are bad people, and there are even good people who do bad things. We know that. We are not oblivious to the fact that some human beings' behavior is disgusting. But I cannot operate at a frequency where I walk around thinking the worst of every single human being. That is a pessimistic state that I don't want to live in, one filled with depression, anxiety, and paranoia.

The life of paranoia is uneasy. It feels like hell to think everyone is going to attack you. And if you truly sit back, observe, and look at reality, you'll see that there have been more people in your life who have caused you no harm than the very few who have caused you harm.

In life, you have already gone through the worst. It has made you stronger, and now you are ready for the best.

— s. mcnutt

You will overcome what you are fighting through. You will find inner peace, and one day this struggle won't feel as strong as it does now. Be patient and keep working toward healing.

— s. mcnutt

When you've been abandoned,
you develop strength within,
but you also don't let people get
close to you.

— s. mcnutt

Being aware of your perspective
matters. If you believe the world
is against you, it will be. If you
believe the world is here for you,
it will be.

— s. mcnutt

Focus on your lane—on your life—and put energy into making your life better.

— s. mcnutt

A person will continue to have toxic connections for two reasons: they have not healed from the pain of previous relationships, and they don't know how to set healthy boundaries.

— s. mcnutt

When we go through madness,
it feels like it will last forever, but
nothing is forever. The pain is
temporary too. It will fade.

— s. mcnutt

I have forgiven everyone who
has caused me pain. Most of
them haven't apologized. I'm
forgiving them because my
healing is more important than
me holding a grudge, which is
more suffering. Healing looks
like forgiving people who have
never apologized—people who
see no harm with what they have
done. Those people have been
removed and will never have
access again. I can work with
someone who is accountable,
who admits that they caused a
fracture. But those who can't,
I can't forgive and let them go.
Forgiveness doesn't mean you
get another chance. Forgiveness
mean we are releasing ourselves
from resentment and choosing to
give properly.

— s. mcnutt

Telling myself, "They did the best they could with what they had" has helped me forgive with compassion. It has helped me let go of yesterday so I can heal and thrive today.

— s. mcnutt

Delete numbers out of your phone, detox your time line, change your routine. Do what needs to be done so you can save yourself. Your healing requires that you have boundaries and let go of what is holding you back.

— s. mcnutt

Unfollow and mute accounts that give you negative energy and play with your emotions. Your online experience is important now. Everyone is fighting for your time and attention. Use these tools wisely. Use them to connect, to be inspired, to have fun with healthy boundaries. Remove yourself from the drama and darkness.

— s. mcnutt

Forgiving someone doesn't mean you're allowing them to come back. It means you're choosing to let go of the pain they once brought. Them coming back is contingent upon changed behavior and acknowledgment of what happened.

— s. mcnutt

Pain has a stickiness factor. You don't want it to stay on you like a scent. You want it to go. Be willing to detox, to shed dead weight, to let go of irrelevant energy.

— s. mcnutt

Choose your words wisely.
Words can be forgiven, but the
impact they have may not be
forgotten.

— s. mcnutt

A Letter to Pain

Hey, pain, I've gotten to know
you well at different parts of my
life, and as much as I want to be
angry with you, I have to thank
you. You taught me how to grow,
how to learn who I am, and most
importantly, how to avoid you.
I am grateful for the people you
have brought me. I am also sorry
because I have hurt people too.
I hope I can be forgiven for my
ways, for the pain that I have
caused too.

— s. mcnutt

In order to heal, we have to be aware of the pain we have caused other people. We have to be willing to apologize and be accountable for it. Empathy and understanding allow us to heal ourselves and teach us how to hold space for those we value.

— s. mcnutt

On Forgiveness

Most people will suffer for the rest of their lives because they're too proud to forgive people who have hurt them. They say things like, "This person doesn't deserve forgiveness." The second you are able to forgive them for what they've done is the second you open a lifetime of healing and peace.

— s. mcnutt

Healing

We heal more when we do not allow our emotions to explode out of control.
The key: learn what and who triggers you, and then practice the art of pausing, breathing deeply, and allowing the outburst to pass.

— s. mcnutt

Cultivate a Healthy Relationship

Create a flowing, open, and judgment-free dialogue. It's not always about having answers. It's truly about having a conversation. Cultivate a space where both people can be unmasked.

— s. mcnutt

Use a healthy tone of voice,
make eye contact, and avoid the
nonverbal cues that show anger
or hostility.

— s. mcnutt

One of the worst mistakes
you can make is to greet your
partner with aggressive, upset,
unruly energy.

If there is an issue, breathe,
relax, and approach them with
compassion.

— s. mcnutt

PROTECTING THE SACRED
GREETING AND EXIT

I am a child of divorced parents. My parents split when I was 14, for the last time. They did the fake breakup at least four times. For the first six to eight years of my life, my parents were happy and did a great job creating our family. I remember walks in the park, parties, movie nights, and bonding over cards and conversation. I was younger, but I was still a hyperaware child, and I didn't feel, nor do I remember, too many vibes that were *off*.

Between the ages of eight and twelve, everything changed. My parents worked so much that when they came home they were so tired. They had nothing left to give us children or each other. Eventually, they just became roommates and stopped greeting each other. There was no excitement when someone came home. We didn't honor anyone anymore. Previously, we would honor each other when someone left or came back. You know how small children are—always excited when people come around whom they like. That childlike spirit that we had in the house began to vanish.

One of the best strategies you can implement in your relationship is to make coming home and leaving home a sacred ritual. Make it a process of honoring the new person or new energy.

Maybe it means the person who comes home walks into a hug, and a kiss on the cheek. Maybe there's a signature handshake. Maybe you're a fit family, and you make each other do three push-ups. We all say now that this may be silly or too much, but if you've ever lost someone before, then you know the only thing we ask for when we lose someone is more time. No matter what, try to protect the greeting and the exit. This part of the daily interactions is sacred. Please cherish it. You never know when it will be the last time you see someone. Make sure the last thought of you is welcome and warm, loving and kind.

What you're unwilling to do
for your partner, another person
will. Focus on learning your
partner's wants and needs as
well as expressing yours. Do not
avoid this.

— s. mcnutt

You should often ask your
partner to express their needs
to you. If they don't tell you,
how can you help fulfill their
experience? This goes both ways.

— s. mcnutt

The emotion of love isn't enough
to keep two people together.
There has to be communication,
compatibility, understanding,
and most importantly, desire on
both ends to keep adding value
to each other's existence.

— s. mcnutt

Make sure you always show
love toward the people you care
about. Life does a great job of
making us mad, and making
us focus on work and school. I
implore you to focus on love, to
focus on giving value to those
you care about.

— s. mcnutt

HOW TO HANDLE BEING TRIGGERED

It is imperative that you deal with your past traumas and pains. If not, you will often operate with some of the most destructive emotions: fear, rage, anxiety, shame, guilt, panic, paranoia, and others.

A healthy adult employs reason and logic, not to the point of going cold and lacking emotion but in conjunction with emotion. Emotion is not bad; it is necessary. But living without control due to emotional spikes can be catastrophic, meaning that relationships can end in a split second because one person can't control his or her behavior or reaction to situations.

As an adult, it is your duty to yourself, to your friends, and to your co-workers to learn how to manage your emotions. I'm not saying to act like they're not there. I am saying evolve to a point where you can suppress your ego, your fears, and the primal negative motivators that make you act like a child when you do not get your way. This is difficult to do, but necessary.

The best advice you'll ever receive on how to manage your emotions is to breathe. Everything about your emotions revolves around how you breathe and your inner dialogue. The next time you lose control, tell yourself to breathe. That is you taking control of your inner dialogue and your emotions.

When you feel yourself becoming triggered, do not ball up your fist. Do not scream and yell at the top of your lungs. Do not fight to be heard. It is possible that the other people around you do not have big enough ears to understand where you're coming from. Do not bicker and make comments under your breath. Do not attack or put them down. Do not throw your alarm clock through the wall, and if you're wondering, I may or may not have done that one time in college. This is my formal apology to my roommates and to the apartment complex for the hole. And to answer your question, yes, we left the alarm clock in the hole, and it hung there all year.

At the end of the day, overreacting will never make the situation better, so it is our goal to understand that before we act. The next time you become super triggered and unruly, make sure you pause, breathe, and gather yourself when these primal, negative emotions take control. This happens to every person, but the most efficient thing to do, in my opinion, is to practice controlling it, and that doesn't mean you have it mastered by midnight tonight. Practice means you take a conscious effort to get better at something, through repetition, coaching, adjusting. Here is a practice that will help you tremendously on your journey. You have to give yourself at least three to five seconds of pure relaxation before you respond to some things, and if you say these words in bold slowly, aloud if possible, this practice will change your life. I have been saying this to myself for 10 years, and each year it gets easier and easier to let things go, to never give my power away. Tell yourself these words: *pause, breathe, and relax.*

Sad, broken, depressed. I've had
the thoughts that run through
your head like a race. "I'm
unworthy." I decided that I didn't
want to be sad. I decided that I
no longer deserved to suffer. I
realized that I am worthy of joy,
of bliss, and happiness, and so
are you. I cried until I ran out of
tears, and then I picked myself
up. I put myself back together.
I fought for myself. I'm not
stronger than you.
We have the same stories; we
are just on two different pages.
Fight through this chapter and
walk away from the pain. You
will overcome these pages. Trust
me, the story turns beautiful
after the ugly.

— s. mcnutt

You will continue to suffer if you
have an emotional reaction to
everything that is said to you.

True power is sitting back
and observing everything with
logic; true power is restraint.
If words control you, that means
everyone else can control you;
breathe and allow things to pass.

— s. mcnutt

You make your life hard by
always being in your head.
Life is simple—get out of your
head and get into the moment.

— s. mcnutt

Most people never heal
because they stay in their
heads, replaying corrupted
scenarios. Let them go.

— s. mcnutt

THREE

LETTING GO

Learning how to let go is a skill. Learning how to and when to let go will save years and years of time. Learning when and how to let go will allow us to put our energy toward the people and activities that matter most to us.

LETTING GO: THE FINAL STEP
TOWARD HEALING FROM PAIN

The final step, and what most people will tell you is the hardest step, of healing from pain is the step called "letting go." I hope I have provided enough value already around understanding, identifying, and reflecting on where the pain comes from and why we hold on. I hope some of the value I gave you around dealing with pain has already helped you let go, and my genuine hope is that this section truly helps you with the closure process that you are craving.

HEALING IS NOT COMPLEX; IT IS SIMPLE

No matter what, always remember this: *healing is a choice*. And once you decide to heal, you will. The last time I wrote about pain in one of my books was about four years ago. In my book *Dear Soul: Love After Pain*, I wrote deeply about all types of pain—how to get through it and how to manage it. In the time that has passed, I haven't experienced very much pain. Some, yes, but I've done a great job of managing the pain that I have experienced, and that is all I want to do with *Care Package*. I want to deliver words, ideas, and strategies that will help you manage new pain as it comes into your life.

Before that book, I lost a relationship, my father, my job, and my identity, and I was in a place of rebuilding. I wrote the book to myself as a way to heal, to face some of the things from my childhood that I dealt with in order to let them go.

Some of my fans have said that my books heal them, and I am grateful for that, but I would never call myself a spiritual healer. Maybe I am one, and I am just in denial. Who knows? I don't have the answer to that question, nor do I need it. I feel like *Care Package* is helping me heal some different pains. I've had to deal with guilt, shame, and codependency, and to be completely honest, the guilt eats me alive. My purpose for writing *Care Package* to myself is to eliminate all this guilt that I have because I know I do not deserve it.

Pain is hard for most people because we define ourselves as pain. We see ourselves as the stories of our past. We lock pain into our minds because we identify with those stories. We judge ourselves in the present moment based on what we experienced before, and we constantly preach to ourselves a level of unworthiness. We take aggressive positions toward our past, cursing at our exes, damning our parents, and holding on to resentment toward an irrelevant person who hurt our feelings years and years ago. All this suffering exists because we lock it into our egos. We lock it into the sense of "me."

My solution for this is to change the narrative. Stop making abuse, pain, and neglect your story. Simply acknowledge that it is a story you experienced. Literally changing your inner dialogue from *This is what happened to me* to *Here is what I learned from this situation* will change how the stories of your past feel.

Healing is a process that starts, occurs, and ends in your mind. Your brain is a tool. If you have used this tool incorrectly in the past, I hope we can change it moving forward. Let's talk deeper about locking pain into your mind and how we can undo it—how we can free the ego and that pain.

Let go of the idea that you're
scared to open up. Life
transforms when you choose
to be brave, to be vulnerable.
To be brave means that you're
scared, that you're the underdog,
but you're still going to give it
everything you have. Opening
up gets energy off your back
and gets you in the space to
receive the healing, counseling,
and support to get through the
road bumps of life. Opening up
may be tough, but if you find
the right people and trust your
healing process, opening up can
welcome in love, healing, and a
new perspective.

— s. mcnutt

Stop negotiating with toxic people. They make you feel crazy for being human. Run away from their energy and save yourself. Toxic people cannot help, love, or serve you in anyway. These people come cloaked as family and friends throughout life. Learn to distance yourself from these people. You are not going to change them, but you can change what you accept and what you allow.

— s. mcnutt

You have to cut off toxic energy as soon as it starts. If you don't, it will get deeper and stronger and will feel normal. Don't play games with toxic energy—at all. Cut it off and be free.

— s. mcnutt

A lot of people go wrong when chaos happens in their lives, because they're rigid. They obsess about going backward, forcing what is broken, and it never works. Instead, embrace the chaos. Believe in staying fluid and adaptable. Never try to change what is happening. Accept reality, and use your skills to adapt to it all.

— s. mcnutt

To let go of the past, stop obsessing about trying to change what happened. Healing occurs when you accept it for what it is.

— s. mcnutt

LEARNING TO FORGIVE SO YOU CAN HEAL

Bitter people will say that the person who hurt them doesn't deserve to be forgiven. If you believe that, you will suffer forever just like they do. It will not be easy to forgive people. We do not practice forgiveness; we practice holding on to pain. We practice reinforcing our egos, and that traps the pain and keeps the cycle going. Forgiveness is the key to breaking the chains of pain that stay locked around your neck. First you have to stop living with your sense of entitlement. You feel like the world owes you everything—every explanation and every action should be in your favor. That's laughable at best. Keeping that mindset will forever enslave you with your pain. Once you accept that nobody owes you anything, which is you freeing your ego, then you can forgive the people who have hurt you. Holding on to pain is a choice, and once you choose to heal, you choose to forgive the people who brought you the pain. This is a process, not a light switch. It is hard because it is the opposite of what we have been taught. Be ready for the challenge—you can do it.

Do you want to stay bitter and hurt, or do you want to heal? Which choice are you going to make? If you forgive your ex, your parent, or even yourself, then you allow the pain to live in the past. Forgiveness allows you to separate the past from the present. Many people do not heal in the now, because they are too identified with the past. They care too much about the story they tell themselves about who they are. The easiest way to ruin your life is to tell yourself stories about the past, to believe these stories, and to box yourself into what those stories tell you about who you are or who you can be.

In the story I gave you, I shared some of the pain I dealt with growing up. I told you how I chose to forgive. I told you how I chose to seek therapy and counseling to help me understand that type of treatment so I could grow from it. Now I do not identify with the pain of the past. I have chosen to forgive my father, my mother, and any person from my past. I don't buy in to self-defeating thoughts about what I can't do, how I'm disadvantaged, or how I am less of a person because of some pain I experienced many years ago. What I just explained to you is the perfect example of why I don't suffer. I don't identify with the pain. It is not locked in my mind. You do not have to suffer either; you do not have to lock it in your mind.

Learning to forgive is a process, but it's easier for you to do once you get out of your ego and get out of your mind.

You cannot rush or expect
to be over pain instantly; it
takes time. Healing is a process,
not a light switch. Don't feel
like you will heal in one day,
for most of it takes years. Allow
your healing process to flow at
the organic pace it deserves. Be
patient with yourself and trust
that it will get better.

— s. mcnutt

Walking Away from Toxic

You stop making excuses for the way they treat you. You realize that their manipulation and games will no longerwork. You become brave enough to walk away and wise enough to stay away.

— s. mcnutt

I genuinely hope you get the happiness you deserve. I hope you have the courage to leave a toxic situation, the strength to recover from one, and the wisdom to know how to avoid them entirely.

— s. mcnutt

I want to remind you that you do not have to tolerate or put up with behavior that is consistently low energy, purposeless, and disrespectful.

Yes, in all relationships there will be conflict. In healthy connections we resolve the conflict and hold space for each other. When you truly love someone or have respect, you hold a certain frame for conflict to be resolved and for healing to occur.

Please be the type of person who tries their best to heal situations. Choose people who are aligned with you and want to heal them as well. We need to be around people who care about reconciliation and closure after conflict.

— s. mcnutt

Letting go means allowing your flesh to shed, your tears to run, and your heart to ache. Not forever, just long enough to wash all the energy off you that no longer deserves to be there.

— s. mcnutt

Let go of the need to be right, the need to prove a point, and the need to prove the truth.

— s. mcnutt

Closure is not going back to the toxic environment that made you sick. If they made you sick, they cannot heal you. Closure is staying away from it, regardless of how bad it keeps trying to bring you back.

— s. mcnutt

And sometimes it's not people that we need to let go of, because it's not them; it's us. Sometimes we have behaviors or mindsets that we have to let go of in order for the ones whom we love to stay around us. If you have been the one to make a mistake, employ a true level of ownership. What's missing in this generation is personal responsibility without complaining or blaming. If you can say, "I made this mistake; I own it and I'm changing behavior," then you will continue to repair your relationships over and over.

— s. mcnutt

Let's be honest: we all make mistakes, and pride has gotten the best of us before. We all have a situation from when we were younger where we didn't take enough accountability. To live inside of mature and integrated relationships, you have to raise your hand when you make a mistake; you must own it. Healing is saying, "I am responsible for this." And a mature partner will see you, will accept your apology, and you both will move forward together.

— s. mcnutt

Let go of the mindset that you never need to leave your neighborhood, your state, your little narrow box. Growth happens when you wander into new spaces. Tasting new cuisines and learning new customs will free you. Seeing new sunsets will help you see the world differently. Take every chance you can to expand your winds, to see what else is going on in the world.

— s. mcnutt

Everything changes. Everyone dies, and we all take losses. Get ahead of the curve and adapt to change, or watch it destroy you.

— s. mcnutt

Stay away from people who think they know everything. Strive to be the type of person who knows that he or she does not know enough.

— s. mcnutt

Healing today is being patient as you work through emotional clutter from yesterday.

— s. mcnutt

Make your life simpler
by reducing how many
decisions you make each day.

Have a morning and night
routine that sets you up to thrive.

Let go of the idea that you
need to make decisions after
the decisions, that's why
people are so tired.

Automate as many
decisions as you can by
creating solid routines.

— s. mcnutt

We hurt ourselves because we
obsess about the end of our
journeys. Focus on staying in the
moment, on being grateful for
where you are today.

— s. mcnutt

Thoughts are seeds; actions are nutrients. What type of garden are you planting?

— s. mcnutt

In life, the only two things you can control are your effort and your attitude. Everything else is not up to you.

— s. mcnutt

FOUR

PEOPLE PLEASING
AND
SETTING
BOUNDARIES

Year after year I used to let people take and take, and I would give and give, and finally I said no. This is my testimony.

CHANGING THE NARRATIVE AROUND
SETTING HEALTHY BOUNDARIES

As children, we do not hear stories about how we should set boundaries between us and other people. The only thing that I remotely remember was "Don't talk to strangers, because strangers are bad." I can see why parents didn't want us to talk to strangers—fear of being kidnapped, fear of an adult overpowering us.

Well, that is actually a flawed mentality. Without talking to strangers, how do we socialize? How do we make friends? How do we find lovers? How do we network and get jobs? "Mom and Dad, if we are not supposed to talk to strangers, how did you two meet to make us?" I said, confused, to my parents. They just looked at me with the "Boy, stop asking questions and just roll with life" face when I was a young kid with a million and one questions.

We are conditioned to keep people away from us. When people walk up to us and introduce themselves because they want a date or find us attractive, typically, we say no. We can be as lonely as hell, wanting a date and companionship, and we'll flat out lie to these strangers who are being vulnerable, because we are conditioned to keep people away from us. We will tell them that we have a boyfriend or girlfriend, knowing that we're lying, when the only thing we have is a liter of wine and a desire to develop partnerships, but we don't, because we are trained to say no to love, to opportunity, to anything that changes our little routines.

The polar opposite of the scenario above is when we completely open up and let people in, but they have shifty morals and crooked intentions—the ones who denigrate us for being human. So here's the real question: Why are we conditioned to keep away strangers? Is it because we fear they may be bad yet we reserve spots for people in our lives who have proven their unfavorable positions?

Is it classical conditioning that keeps us running back to people who may not be good for us? Is it our inherent sense of family or loyalty that makes us stay committed to people who are truly toxic? Do you follow where I am going here? Doesn't it seem hypocritical that we are so fearful and wary of *strangers*, but we are welcoming of all the *people we know*, even when their actions are egregious, abusive, and malicious?

I believe we have to find some balance with this mindset. There are some strangers who for sure need to be let into our lives. Sometimes our soul mate is sitting right across from us at the coffee shop, and we never stop to say hello. So it seems that we have to find balance by being willing to allow strangers into our little bubbles. No, not everyone, and not whenever the hell they want, but more often than we are accustomed to. And the other side of that balance is taking these people that we know—whom we love, whom we break bread with, who drive us insane—and figuring out how to implement barriers, boundaries, and a code of conduct for how we will and will not be treated. If you struggle with setting boundaries, this section will shine light on the elements of the practice that I feel are necessary to live an effective and happy life, a life that allows you to remain open to new friends and strangers but also doesn't allow you to get used and abused by familiar faces. But first, let me start off with a story.

THIS IS WHY YOU HAVE
TO SET BOUNDARIES

I received a phone call one day from someone who was asking me for almost $2,000 to help cover his monthly finances. I looked at my phone like it was an April Fool's joke. I couldn't believe what I was hearing—a grown adult asking me to cover monthly expenses for him while he sat in his air-conditioned apartment with cable, Wi-Fi, and a brand new car sitting in the driveway. As my mother used to always say, "Excuse me, but you have me fucked up." What he had asked me for was unreasonable. Two thousand dollars is a month of my living expenses: rent, gas, food, etc. I didn't feel comfortable giving away a month of my savings, and to be clear, I was offended that this was the question.

This was after another person had asked me for $600 to help his financial shortcomings; again, this was another adult. That was right after someone else had asked me for $950 to help him with a down payment on something he could afford, also another adult. I had to ask myself, after having this very intense 10-to-12-day period, *Why the hell do people keep asking me for these big sums of money like I'm the Monopoly Man?*

I'm an entrepreneur, a writer. I work hard for my money. It's 4:11 A.M., and I'm up writing about a subject I'm passionate about. I don't understand why they're not up grinding like I am. I work hard for myself, for my brand, and if I get a part-time job again, I will work hard for that company. I am not trying to imply that others are not working hard. I am not saying that I am better than anyone or that anyone else is less than I am. I am saying that I choose to live a less fancy life than some people. I choose not to buy fancy clothes. I choose not to get animals. I choose not to get a car note. I am a minimalist who owns 10 pairs of jeans and about 15 shirts. I don't have cable. I don't pay monthly subscriptions for magazines, and now I get my hair done at home instead of the barbershop or salon. I don't buy Starbucks; I get the K-cups from Safeway. I have a monthly budget, and giving money to people who live above their means, who don't use a budget and will simply be asking for it again, is no longer a part of my plan for success. I have to say no. I have to *set boundaries*. I cannot *people please*. I do not feel *guilt* for saying no either. (Chapter titles of *Care Package*. Did you catch that?)

Plus, there is another side of this. I remember when I needed to borrow $1,000 from friends. When I got on the phone with them, I had a plan. I had dates, and I had proof that I would pay them back in fewer than six weeks. I needed $1,000, so I asked two friends for $500 each. I told them about the new job I was offered and how it was 60 miles from my residence. They both understood that I needed a new vehicle to ensure that I could make it to this new career. I was living within my means and wasn't asking for money because I was living bigger than my income. My salary was going from about $300–$400 a week as a server and chef to a salary of $28,000 plus commission, as a salesperson. Part of the reason I turned them down is because they didn't have a plan, a way to ensure that my money would come back. Part of the reason I was comfortable asking for money when I needed it was because I had a plan. I had an opportunity for new income, and I knew I wasn't going to buy things I didn't need. It was 100 percent a need. The second time I needed money was when my father died, and I needed $380 to buy a plane ticket. My cousins put the money together, and I paid them back within a month. I am not into owing people. I am not into people having the upper hand on me. When I die nobody will say that I owe them, but everyone will say that I gave something to them or that I did something for them. This is a conscious choice.

Phrases to Say to Help You Set Boundaries

"To be completely honest, that is my personal business, and it is none of your business."

"This is not a threat. I'm just communicating. If you continue to treat me in this way, then I will have to do _____ to protect myself."

"No, I cannot allow you to treat me like this. I do not deserve this. I can't stand for it."

"The last time was the last time that I'll ever be a part of something like that. We do not treat each other like that."

"I've never talked to you with that tone or with those words. We don't talk to each other like that. You cannot speak to me that way."

"What you're asking me to do is simply outside of what I feel comfortable with."

Six Tips on How to Stop People Pleasing Right Now

1. Realize, accept, and understand that this behavior is actually hurting you no matter how much you think you are helping another person.

2. Realize, accept, and understand that this behavior is enabling other people's negative ways instead of encouraging them to grow.

3. Tell yourself that you don't want to feel drained or used any longer.

4. Tell yourself that it is possible to find people who appreciate you—people who do not make you go against yourself.

5. Ask yourself this and answer honestly: If I tell them no, will they be okay? If I tell them yes, even though I want to say no, will I be okay?

6. People pleasing only stops once you stop it. Why would they purposely tell you to stop giving them the benefits that you're willing to provide? The power has always been with you to say no, and once you do, your life will change.

Four Incredible Tips on How to Set Boundaries

1. You have to know what you want, how you want to be treated, and what you deserve to get out of a situation. You'll never stick up for yourself if you don't know why you're doing it in the first place, so know what you want.

2. Communicate that you have been violated, used, or abused. Be very direct, and do not try to spare feelings. It is important that the seriousness of this violation is understood. Be tactful in your execution of explaining this. Communicate with love, and watch your tone.

3. Make suggestions for how a person should treat you. Give them a real-life example of what is okay and what is not, real or hypothetical.

4. They always say treat people how you want to be treated, but it's deeper than that. Show people how you will or will not be treated by having the power and will to walk away the second it turns abusive, violent, aggressive, or anything that is outside of your boundaries.

Three Principles on Setting Boundaries That Matter Today

1. Nobody is going to meet you in a place that you haven't met yourself. Nobody is going to all of a sudden say, "Hey, let me respect you when you don't respect you." You must always meet yourself at the level of consciousness that you want other people to meet you at.

2. Assess your boundaries often. You may have set them, but things change, people change, and situations change. It may be time for you to adjust and adapt to a new set of rules for yourself.

3. Remain open-minded, and stay open to change because a boundary doesn't mean forever. A boundary that you set doesn't mean everyone has to follow or abide by it. Sometimes your boundary can be unfair and can put too much pressure on people, so always check yourself as you set them.

You show others how to
treat you based on how you
allow yourself to be treated.

— s. mcnutt

People respect you more
if you stand up for yourself,
if you have a backbone.

— s. mcnutt

Walking away from a toxic situation is a form of setting a boundary. It's your way of saying, "I will not settle for a poisonous situation."

— s. mcnutt

To vibrate higher, we have to be okay with being alone, with being patient while we attract the right energy.

— s. mcnutt

Self-love is about participating
in healthy environments that
nourish you and help you grow.
It is also about cutting yourself
off from evil and energy-draining
environments that kill you slowly.

— s. mcnutt

Nobody will tell you to set
boundaries. All the people
around you benefit from your
giving nature. Check yourself
and slow down if you're
giving too much.

— s. mcnutt

You push people up because your heart is strong. Be careful pulling the ones who pull you down.

— s. mcnutt

When people treat you like you're garbage, look them right in the eye and say, "I am not the one," and then walk away.

— s. mcnutt

Be intentional about setting a standard for how you will and will not be treated.

Set your boundaries and stick to them so others know how to treat you.

Set boundaries today, and your heart will thank you tomorrow.

— s. mcnutt

I was 18 years old. My father kicked me out of the house, rather violently, and I had nowhere to go.

My resources were short, and my experience wasn't long. I sat there with a bag of my stuff and some four-year-old gym shoes, and I asked myself, *What am I going to do now?* It was in that moment of weakness that I became my strongest.

I told myself that I would work for what I want, that I would become a boss, that I wouldn't allow anyone to have that much control over me ever again. It taught me that crying isn't going to help, and creating abundance, financially and spiritually, was my only option.

— s. mcnutt

When I depended on other people for shelter, food, clothing, and permission, I was always at their mercy. I had to live in their house and abide by their rules, physically and emotionally, and that's not a mental prison that I deserved to live in. I bossed up.

I put myself first so I could live freely without feeling trapped or chained. I set a boundary with myself: I wouldn't allow any human to control me like they were God.

— s. mcnutt

When you have a near-death experience, all you think about is life. All you want is more time and opportunity so you can live right. Some of the people in your life are near-death experiences. Allow them to teach you that you need to live your life more . . . and stress, worry, and waste time less.

— s. mcnutt

If you take the trash out of the kitchen and leave it by the door, what happens? Your entire house stinks. Don't cut off toxic energy halfway. If you're going to get rid of it, get rid of it fully.

— s. mcnutt

Never take it personally if I need time to myself. I don't always know how to communicate that I want to be alone. People are so offended these days.

— s. mcnutt

The hardest people to set boundaries with are family members. Most passionate people are raised to think that you have to always be there for family members because that's what *real love* is about.

Sometimes making people be there for themselves is more important than you being there for them. We have to ask ourselves: *"Am I really helping them, or am I enabling them to keep doing wrong and harm?"* It's hard to say no to them, but at times it's very necessary.

— s. mcnutt

As you get older, you cannot settle for things you used to settle for. Connections change because what you require out of your interactions changes.

Explaining this to someone from your past is not always easy because it's hard for people to see growth in others.

Don't guilt yourself if you have to end a connection because they're not respecting your growth. Maybe they'll come back around when they're ready to vibrate at your level, or maybe they won't.

— s. mcnutt

I hurt myself by breaking
my back for others, by giving
and giving when nothing was
coming back.

I've decided that the people
who used to use me have to
be cut off or understand that
I've changed.

The old me died yesterday,
and I have gone through a
rebirth today. Don't say you
know me until you get to know
the new me. As of today, you
just *knew* me.

— s. mcnutt

Be More Selfish

If you're a giver, always
looking out for others,
always feeling drained
because you break yourself
so others can stay together,
take a break from it. Add
value to your own life first.
Add self-love and peace
to your life first.

— s. mcnutt

People pleasing is an ugly
trait. How can they respect
you if you don't respect yourself?
How can they grow with you
if all you do is break yourself
for other people?

— s. mcnutt

A Letter on People Pleasing

First off, pat yourself on the back because you're the type of person who will continue to give and give to people around you, and there's no shame in that. Secondly, you have finally realized that not everyone deserves the blessing of your presence—of your giving—and that is perfectly okay too. You've grown so much. You require more of people, but at the core of who you are, you still want to give first, and that makes you beautiful. Find people who appreciate you, who can meet you with your giving and smile at all the lives you impact.

— s. mcnutt

On Putting Yourself First

Finally, you have learned and accepted that nobody will ever tell you to take care of you first. Most people care about themselves and their experience, so how can they tell you to take care of you and your experience? We are all living for ourselves until we make beautiful children or until we find a lover who feels like the summertime. And even with them, you still have to learn how to say no, how to change relationships when people take advantage of you, and how to have a backbone when it matters. The world is a tough place if and only if you do not stand up for yourself, and even when you do, others may still find ways to try to pull you down. And what you have to always remember is that what other people do is not up to you. You cannot control it, and you need to simply concern yourself with you and your behavior. Set the boundaries that you need to set and trust the process. It will work out in your favor.

— s. mcnutt

FIVE

GUILT

The definition of guilt: *a feeling of deserving blame for offenses.*

VULNERABLE STORY ON GUILT

Way back in the day, I used to work in the nightclub industry. Yes, pre-social media boom I was one of the best marketers out there. I was twenty-one years old, the age when most people hit the clubs. I loved the experience because it taught me to value genuine connections. Yes, you can meet good people there, but for the most part everything in that industry is fake; it's all a facade. Of course, you learn this with time, with experience, with alertness, but I didn't know this at first.

I worked there because like any other person fresh out of college, I was in debt, broke, and just trying to get a footing in the world. That's all I was trying to do—network, grow, connect, and get paid. I had many friends who would go with me—friends who worked in the industry and people who would link up every so often, but they weren't friends.

One of my close friends made many poor decisions with me when we were young. Many nights were spent nursing each other because of too much alcohol, and many mornings were spent eating tacos and nachos at five o'clock.

In Chicago there was this spot named Taco Burrito King, and I should be part owner for all the times I've invested in their company as a drunk twentysomething. I like to refer to these episodes as the "I'm broke financially but rich in experience" period of our lives, also known as the "I'm young, so I'm going to do stupid stuff" time.

Of course, you would love to see people in their early twenties have secure careers and find themselves, but I am grateful I had a little stupid fun when I was younger. I feel like we are so controlled and limited that we never get to know ourselves until we are in our twenties. College, high school, and living with your parents are all very restrictive, controlled, and for the most part, limiting and confining. How are people supposed to find themselves when they've never been alone, never been allowed to fail, and never learned from people outside their bloodline? Point being, this sacred time put me in the nightclubs after college, talking to women who acted like they were too good for anyone and trying to outdo the next guy who didn't have any money either—the irony. Part of the reason I worked at the clubs was so I did not have to pay to get in—duh. But what do you think happened? What always happens: *it got old*. I outgrew it. I got tired of dealing with energy that didn't vibrate with me, and I removed myself from that environment.

When I moved on, I really moved on. I stopped drinking. I stopped partying. I stayed off the scene. No bars. No clubs. No girls. Nothing. Just me and my solitude. Me and my new job that I loved. I was fortunate enough to put myself in a situation where I had a salary and commission in my new sales career away from the city, tucked away in a little suburb called Wheaton, Illinois. It was my first "big-boy" job, as they say, and I didn't want to blow it because I was out partying too much. Time out: to be truthful and transparent here, I still went once I got the job, just not as much.

As I settled in to this new job, I slowly faded out of the scene. One day I was all work and no play, which was fine, because I was all play and no work at one point. As I grew and matured, my friends didn't advance at my pace, and as you grow, you will experience the exact same thing. When you see that you've outgrown situations, friends, and behaviors that now seem toxic, you look at them with a strange eye when everyone else thinks they're normal. That is how you know that you are going through a spiritual awakening.

HOW THE GUILT STARTED DURING
MY SPIRITUAL AWAKENING

As I started to fade away from the scene, the people who needed me to go to the clubs kept calling. The ones who benefited from my extroversion called and texted. The women who wanted to use my power for free drinks, discounted bottles, or attention at the hottest clubs kept calling. The guys who wanted to use me because there was always a pretty girl or group of them around me kept calling, and what do you think happened?

I went back. Not because I wanted to but because like you, I didn't understand that I was a people pleaser. Even though some of these connections were weak and fleeting, fake and disingenuous; even though these environments caused me pain, didn't bring me joy, and left me drained, I still went because I wanted to please other people. Once you feel that type of inner guilt, that is the exact moment you have to take control of your life.

When you're young, you may not get this. You may act young, silly, goofy, and you might not take life seriously, which is fine. Be carefree, but the moment you realize that you're outgrowing things, be ready to distance yourself from friends; otherwise they will suck you back in. You're going to say yes because you don't take yourself seriously enough, and truthfully, you may not be just a young person who has this issue. You can be in your fifties and still have this struggle. I just had a book reading in Phoenix, and most of the people there were in their late twenties to midthirties. Even people in the middle of their lives have trouble saying no to friends, family, and co-workers.

You have the boss who always asks you to stay late. Even though you can't, you stay anyway. You stay because you haven't read what we talked about in the last chapter: saying no and setting boundaries. In my situation, I tried my best to distance myself, to stay away, but I never set boundaries. I never said no because it was what I meant. I was only able to say no once another person would feel my guilt and let me off the hook. I don't want you to wait until other people let you off the hook. I want you to learn this now.

You will outgrow people. It will confuse them, and when this happens you have to realize that the friendship may truly be over. Do not allow people from your past to guilt you into what you used to do and who you used to be if those behaviors cause you pain. You don't have to go back to being the person who you want to be just because your old friends want you to return there. You can say no, you can turn them down, and you can ascend to new heights without going back to your old ways. If you are struggling with ascending, feeling like you're not being a good friend or partner, it's probably because you're dealing with an inner dialogue that isn't helpful.

How to Deal with Inner Guilt

1. Realize and accept that you do not have to
    own the guilt. It's not your responsibility.

2. You feel guilty because you outgrew people,
    but that's a normal process that occurs in life,
    and you should look at growth as a positive
    experience, not a negative one.

3. It's not your responsibility to ensure that
    other people grow, especially other adults,
    because we are all in charge of ourselves.

4. Realize that acting like a superhero will
    always hurt you. Help people when you
    can. Show up when you can, but you're not
    obligated to do everything or be everywhere
    for everyone else all the time.

5. Life has always been and will always be
    the survival of the fittest. Those who grow,
    who adapt, who get stronger and wiser, and
    who adjust their behavior are the ones who
    will live happily. If other human beings
    consciously choose not to evolve, don't
    feel like it's your fault they didn't or your
    responsibility to make them.

Phrases to Help Communicate Guilt as You Feel It So You Can Let It Go in That Moment

"If I could help you, I would. But at this moment, I am unable to."

"I'm sorry to hear what you're going through. What actions have you taken to fix/solve this?"

"I want to understand where you're coming from right now. Are you venting to me, or are you asking me for help?"

"I know pride might be killing you, but if you need help, you must communicate it directly to me. I do not understand the indirect gestures."

"I am not in a position to help."

"I do not have the ability to help."

"I know for a fact that you'll get through this situation. If I could do more, I would. But I am unable to fulfill that request."

You will outgrow people. It will confuse them. No matter what, stay on your path.

— s. mcnutt

Everyone has to save themselves from their own messes.

— s. mcnutt

Don't say anything negative about yourself just because others do. Another person's opinion of you is not a fact.

— s. mcnutt

Remember this: everyone else is scared, everyone else is trying to figure out who they are, and most people give up on their dreams. Don't listen to them.

— s. mcnutt

Empaths Who Give Too Much

You have such a big heart that it causes you to get in your own way sometimes. You lend a helping hand before people ask you for it. You feel guilt and discomfort when you're unable to help. You go out of your way all the time when others don't go out of their way for you or even themselves. You give like it's your job. You support friends. You are a good person, but if you're feeling guilty because you can't be there, it's okay.

You have spent your entire life being in everyone's corner, and you've reached that point in your life where you need to be there for yourself. Save yourself this time.

— s. mcnutt

A Letter on Guilt

When I was younger, I was given phrases and teachings like everyone else: Don't be too loud. Be nice to people. Be kind. Always help people out if you can, especially family. And now that I am older, I don't believe in any of that blindly. I help if I can help. I risk my life, my resources, or what I have going on only when I am able to. I will not break myself, my bank account, my mental health, or my peace of mind just because I need to save someone. I believe in people learning from their mistakes like I did. I want to help. By nature I am giving, but I am no longer married to the guilt that comes with saying no. I have divorced the guilt that comes from walking away from commitments that used to be great but have since turned poor. Now I live by this: save yourself. That doesn't mean I am heartless, don't care, or will not help. It simply means that I do care, but I have to always check and double-check before I risk breaking my inner peace.

— s. mcnutt

How You Know You're Going through a Spiritual Awakening

- It feels like you've outgrown situations, friends, and behaviors that were once normal because now they seem toxic to you.

- What society has accepted as normal is actually strange to you.

- You stop caring about fitting in.

- You accept that you were born to stand out, to build your own path.

Toxic environments do not
create healthy people. You may
have overcome the worst, but
to reach your best, you have to
heal from the pain those toxic
environments created.

— s. mcnutt

You can say no, you can turn
them down, and you can ascend
to new heights without going
back to your old ways. If they
don't like it, let them deal with
their inner conflicts.

— s. mcnutt

Stand your ground. If you're not
comfortable with the situation,
say no. Life goes on.

— s. mcnutt

Don't give fourth and fifth
chances for people to keep
hurting you like they did the
first, second, and third time.
Be forgiving but not stupid.
These aren't mistakes. This
is true behavior. Don't feel
guilty for walking away from
destructive behavior.

— s. mcnutt

If you look back objectively
and feel like you did everything
you could, then you do not
deserve to allow the guilt to
eat you alive today.

— s. mcnutt

MAKING GUILT LIGHTER
SO YOU CAN GET RID OF IT!

We aren't done talking about guilt. This is one of the most important subjects I'll ever write about. After writing this entire book, I realized I was holding on to a massive amount of guilt, and holding on to guilt was stopping me from moving forward. *Care Package* helped me greatly. I hope you're getting value out of these vulnerable stories, poems, and quotes.

Who will run faster: you carrying 300 pounds or you carrying 100 pounds? Of course you will move faster carrying something lighter, because the mass is much smaller. Think of guilt like an extra 200 pounds.

It's dangerous to your life, and it's dangerous to your progress. In fact, it keeps you on a constant plateau. It keeps you in a state of fear, a state of anxiety.

Understanding how guilt works will help you understand codependency. It will help you understand why you don't set boundaries. It will help you understand how to love yourself deeper. These topics are all intertwined, and that is why *Care Package* is the most important book I've written.

In *Lust For Life*, I talked about developing abundance. I talked about getting on a budget and saving money. I talked about building your business or getting promoted at the job. I talked about how you deserve to experience life and to be rich in experience, but there is another element that comes with that, which is something I am truly experiencing now that is rooted in guilt. Right now I want to talk to you about survivor's guilt and how unbundling guilt will help you reach more abundance in life.

Survivor's Guilt

A modern-day example of survivor's guilt occurred in the movie *The Hunger Games*. If you observe Katniss, the protagonist, you can see that she suffers immensely with survivor's guilt. She is haunted and corrupted by the deaths she causes and the deaths she is around through the *Hunger Games* elimination competitions.

The universe is always in alignment, and I watched all four movies for the first time the weekend just before writing this. It's ironic to me that while I am writing about guilt, I observe a protagonist who suffers greatly from survivor's guilt—a protagonist who helped me understand myself and my life deeper. *The Hunger Games* is like *The Matrix* trilogy, a movie series that has deeper analogies related to our society, about how we are conditioned, and how we treat one another. These films use entertainment to make us think about ourselves.

Survivor's guilt is an experience a person feels when he or she survives something traumatic. I can flat-out tell you that this is something I have dealt with my entire life. I am from Chicago, and all we know is struggle. Being a black man in a country that still doesn't like black men is traumatic. Every day I have to walk around and make sure I'm less threatening or prove to people that I am no danger to them, because the media loves to paint distorted images of black men. When you look back in time, you'll see the movie *Black Panther* is one of the greatest movies of all time, and it's mostly an all-black cast that broke the stereotypical roles given to black actors. I don't have the platform that Hollywood has, but one of my underlying goals with my social media, with my brand, and with my books is to control my narrative, to show you that we destroy stereotypes where I come from.

I was involved in a school shooting where six people were killed (NIU, Valentine's Day 2008). I've watched my friends be abused by their parents, and we thought it was normal. The first three girlfriends I had were all raped or sexually abused when they were younger, and so I grew up thinking that all women went through sexual abuse.

Think about someone who is born into slavery. They'll have a hard time desiring freedom because they may not know that it is even possible. I was conditioned to all this stuff, and it made me cold. It made me savage, and it made me not trust anyone from my environment.

In Chicago, where I'm from, it's everyone against everyone. There is no love. It felt like I was in a war outside of the house, dealing with racism, mean girls, and teachers who never let me express myself when I was a child. Combine all that with what I had to go through at home: two parents who were verbally abusive, physically coercive, and emotionally absent. I've lived through hell already, in my opinion.

Both parents being emotionally unavailable was one of the key components that led me down the path toward becoming a writer. There was no one for me to have an open-ended conversation with. Everything in my household was manipulated, judged, or controlled. There was no freedom to simply be who I was. As a result, they created an angry child who felt like he had to survive—a child who felt like he had no friends, couldn't trust anyone, and if he didn't save himself, then nobody would be there for him. This is what I dealt with, and it's who I was.

I had the "me against the world" mindset—survivor's mindset, warrior mindset. People who have come from similar backgrounds are often the hardest workers because we try to create a new identity through our work. We are often great at sports or music because we always have constant inspiration to draw from. People like me are often closed off and unwilling to open up, something *Care Package* is helping us do.

Look back on the profile I described. I am certainly not that person today. I am not those stories today. I am simply shining a light on a level of consciousness that I once had, to help you see the contrast between what happened to me and what is happening to me, so we can dissect what survivor's guilt truly is.

One of the reasons why you read my work, in my little opinion, is because I've been through hell and survived. I've been through so much pain, and yet my message is love. My message is healing. My message is that we can overcome, and that inspiration is what everyone needs in their lives. I believe that is the reason why you have found me among others.

Today I am happy. I have forgiven. I have made peace with so much and moved forward. I have been able to help millions of people do the same thing.

I feel rich. I don't know what other people consider rich, but I feel rich. I have no debt. I own my car. I have money in my emergency fund. I have investments. I am intentional about keeping my income high and my expenses low. I am focused on living as simply as possible and not buying excessive things. I am not into consumerism. I am into living below my means and remaining grateful for what I have.

I have healthy relationships and friendships. I have healthy habits; I practice yoga and weight lifting. I am mindful and minimal with my possessions. I have a job I like and a life I love. I get a lot of fulfillment out of the life that I live. I have found my passion, which is to be vulnerable and to use my talent to inspire people. I have found my passion, which is to take care of my health and to have fun. I have found my passion, which is to invest time and energy into relationships, to travel, and to eat new foods often.

And this is where survivor's guilt creeps in.

You say to yourself, *Damn, why did I make it through, and they didn't?* You end up asking yourself why you were luckier or more fortunate than the others who died when they were put in the same situation as you.

You look at your brother and sister and friends and family and wish they could feel what you feel or that they could be blessed the way you are, and that is when the guilt permeates your body. You want to travel, to live, to smile, and you see people you're close to in depression, broke, and run-down. So you ask yourself why you were chosen to win. To answer that question, you have found *Care Package*.

Do a job you like. Build a
life you love.

— s. mcnutt

You can find a lot of value
and purpose within the work
you do. Show up on time, put
value into your work, and
always be willing to learn.

— s. mcnutt

One of the keys of power
is to always control your own
narrative: don't let others
tell your side of the story.

— s. mcnutt

How are people supposed to
find themselves when they've
never been alone, never been
allowed to fail?

— s. mcnutt

Life is a mix of victories and defeats. Appreciate the victories and learn from the defeats. Stay humble through all the winning, and never turn against yourself when you take losses.

— s. mcnutt

Note to Self:

You are only responsible for your own experience. Save yourself. Be the hero you need for you today, tomorrow, and every day thereafter.

— s. mcnutt

Never stay in a relationship only because you're afraid you will hurt them more by breaking up. That is the wrong reason to stay together. You're hurting yourself more and more each day. They are responsible for their feelings and healing process, not you.

— s. mcnutt

Learning to not guilt-trip yourself might be hard, but it is not impossible.

— s. mcnutt

We feel guilt when we say no because we are used to feeling like we are obligated to be a superhero, and we feel obligated to save people from their own problems. Saying no does not make you a villain. In fact, if you want to survive this life, you'll have to be your own hero and practice the art of saving yourself.

— s. mcnutt

All you can do is be yourself, present the most organic version of yourself, and allow the rest to play itself out. You are not responsible for what people do or do not understand.

— s. mcnutt

SIX

CODEPENDENCY

I was codependent. I was codependent. I was codependent. This is how I broke out of it and how you can too.

I came from a dysfunctional home, a home that had two alcoholics, a home that shut down feelings and tough conversations. That kind of energy produces a deep level of codependency.

Many people have codependent behaviors, and they never realize it. Understanding codependency and taking action to prevent it not only manifests healthy relationships but can also help you leave toxic ones.

Being able to identify codependency can stop you from jumping into cycles of pain, cycles of mistrust, and cycles of pure dysfunction. In *Codependent No More*, Melody Beattie loosely gives these words as a way to identify codependency: if concern has turned into obsession; if compassion has turned into caretaking; or if you are taking care of other people and not taking care of yourself, you may be struggling with codependency. Each person must decide for themselves if codependency is a problem. Each person must decide for themselves what needs to be changed and when that should happen. People who grow up with alcoholics, are friends with people who have eating disorders, or are friends with severely insecure people often fall into codependency. They fall into the trap of trying to save someone, even if it means they lose themselves in the process. The term is vague because it's truly up to people to determine for themselves if they are indeed codependent, and once they do, then and only then can they adjust behavior. Beattie goes on to say, "As far as an origin of the word goes, professionals had long suspected something peculiar happened to people who were closely involved with chemically dependent people."[2]

Personally, I grew up with two alcoholic parents, and as a result, I became an adult who often thought he needed to save people, who needed to care about people's results more than they do. And if I was not *helping* people, then I was not fulfilled, because it felt like it was my duty to help. That is the inner dialogue of codependency. After being objective and honest with myself and doing a lot of reflecting, I saw that I needed to break up with those mindsets. Like you, I thought to myself, *Well, people are going to think I don't care and that I am some savage if I am not jumping in helping them.* Here's what I realized: it doesn't matter what people think about you. What matters is what you think about you. It's hard to come to that agreement with yourself at first because codependency has taught us that saving the world is just more important than saving ourselves, and it's not. In fact, you will save the world if you save yourself. You will change the world if you change yourself. And that's the part that we do not get when we are blindly following codependent behaviors. Once I elevated myself, made barriers and boundaries, my friendships and connections changed. I met new people who cared about valuing me and cherishing me. The old people who had been there when I was Superman stepped up to the challenge of meeting my new energy.

Some people faded away because they simply couldn't vibrate at this new level, but that is okay. Not everyone can stay around once you elevate. I'm willing to bet my next cup of water that if you elevated yourself, you would have the same effect. You would make people treat you better simply because you treated yourself better. Freeing yourself from codependency, in my opinion, all starts in your mind, and then gets executed through a change in behavior. In order to change behavior, we have to change mindset. Changing mindset is all about seeing the value of the change or adjustment. I cannot tell you why you need to stop being codependent. But for me, I wanted to stop saving people. I wanted to stop hurting myself. I wanted to free myself of guilt. I wanted to look out for me first because nobody else was. I wanted to use my hard-earned resources for my life.

Activity to Help Attack Codependency

1. Do some independent research on what codependency is to you because *your* definition of it matters too.

2. Write down an action plan. Identify which behaviors you do that you do not like, and create a plan to work on reducing them until you reach the point where you can get rid of them.

3. Use a daily journal to write your experiences. Doing this will allow you to go back and see your stories and experiences and eventually learn from them.

The number one thing I had to stop doing was trying to jump in and save people from their own decisions. I had to realize that saving people is enabling them to do it again. I was hurting more than I was helping.

— s. mcnutt

Codependency has taught us that saving the world is more important than saving ourselves, and it's not. In fact, you will save the world if you save yourself.

— s. mcnutt

Are you really saving someone
else if you lose yourself during
the process of helping them?

— s. mcnutt

They may never speak of
the hard times they're going
through. All they need is an ear
that will listen, a hug, and to
know someone cares deeply.

— s. mcnutt

Life is survival of the fittest.
If people are doing things that
are killing them, that doesn't
mean you have to participate.
Save yourself.

— s. mcnutt

If you fight for it, I'll fight with
you. If you don't want to fight for
it, then I have to find someone
who wants it as badly as I do.

— s. mcnutt

Stop begging people to call you back, to respond to your texts, to like you, to commit to you, and to be your friend. That's fake.

When the connection is genuine, you never have to beg someone for attention or respect.

— s. mcnutt

Break up with the behavior of
chasing adults who don't want
to communicate. Life is too short
to waste precious energy with
them, when there are adults who
love to communicate.

— s. mcnutt

I enjoy being alone. I'm not
lonely when I'm alone. I'm
just in "my zone." The right
people and energy will easily
bring me out of my zone. If they
have the wrong energy for me,
then I'd rather stay in my zone.

— s. mcnutt

Stop Doing This

Some people never move on from an ex because they keep having that *maybe-sex-will-bring-us-back-together* sex. You will never move on from an ex if you keep opening up to him or her. Stop it. Close the door. Delete the number. Block the contact. Don't mistake great sex for relationship compatibility and healthy connection.

— s. mcnutt

You'll never move on from someone if you keep investing in him or her when history has proven that there is no return on that investment.

— s. mcnutt

You swear up and down that your ex is the worst human being around; however, you keep going back.

— s. mcnutt

PART II

TREATING YOURSELF WITH LOVE AND COMPASSION

SEVEN

SELF-CARE AND PUTTING YOURSELF FIRST

I just heard a girl list the top 10 things in her life that she cares about most, and she didn't list herself.

This is the problem we are dealing with.

How you treat yourself today
is the blueprint for how others
will treat you tomorrow.

— s. mcnutt

If you treat yourself well
and there are people who
are committed to treating
you like trash, at some point
you have to acknowledge
that their behavior isn't about
you, and it's a reflection of
them. Walking away is your
duty at this point.

— s. mcnutt

Remove yourself from people who treat you like your time doesn't matter, like your feelings are worthless, or like your soul is replaceable.

— s. mcnutt

Everything in life works out in your favor once you take care of yourself.

Hydrate, stretch, sleep enough, connect with your lover, eat healthy food, and take care of your mind and body, no matter what.

— s. mcnutt

Healing Is Important

We experience trauma directly through our experiences and indirectly by empathizing with friends, the news, and even strangers. We owe it to ourselves to seek healing—therapy, detoxes, moments of solitude, physical fitness, etc.

— s. mcnutt

TOP 10 SECRETS TO IMPLEMENTING TRUE SELF-LOVE TODAY

1. Care less about others' opinions.

2. Tell yourself positive affirmations daily, not to create delusion but to create inner support.

3. Understand that it's okay to be aware of what you dislike about yourself, but that doesn't mean you have to beat yourself up about it.

4. Take time for yourself every day and be selfish with your energy and time.

5. Tell people no if it's hurting you, breaking you, draining you, or causing unruliness.

6. Say yes to something new—experiences, opportunities, people, life, ideas, hobbies.

7. Delete all the sad songs off your playlist and jam out to new ones—the ones that make you dance, the ones that make you laugh and party.

8. Take a self-care day, which might involve the following: spa, haircut, gym, massage, sauna, chiropractor, yoga, nails, hairstyle.

9. Give love to others without expecting it back. This is also a form of self-love.

10. Celebrate the small victories when you grow, mature, or overcome something.

Do not break yourself by trying
to keep someone else together.
If I have to go out of my way
to keep your life together, to
keep you ticking, to keep you
motivated for your own goals,
then that means you are my
dependent child, and I will do
everything in my power to help
you. If you are not my child, do
not get mad when I tell you to
deal with your own life. I will
not break myself to keep another
adult together.

— s. mcnutt

Avoid people who always have bad things happen to them. They are attracting it more than they know.

— s. mcnutt

In the long run, the people who succeed a little often succeed a lot. The people who keep losing in life get used to losing: proof that mindset plus action is everything.

— s. mcnutt

Embracing Boundaries

This new you knows how to set boundaries; this new you knows how to run away from energy that is corrupt and evil.

— s. mcnutt

I set healthy boundaries with people now. I am unwilling to surround myself with dark energy just because other people are okay with it. I am okay alone. I am okay with walking far distances, literally or figuratively, in order for me to escape that energy.

— s. mcnutt

Stop pouring your heart into the heartless. Don't spend any more time on unrequited love. Pouring energy into someone who doesn't pour it into you only drains you. There is a person who will appreciate your love— one who doesn't want to drain you, one who wants to give back. Find that soul.

It's okay to pour your heart out into other people; however, self-love teaches you that even the biggest giver still needs it to come back. It's not selfish to want love back—it's human.

— s. mcnutt

Tell your lover that it's okay to tell you no. Tell your lover that they should not break their back for you if they don't have to. If you truly have a great partner, tell them that your goal is to be a great partner too, and that you never want them to feel used or overworked.

— s. mcnutt

Sometimes you need time alone to do things for yourself that make your life better. This is called self-care and recharging. Take time to add value back into yourself.

— s. mcnutt

When you need self-care time, communicate it, and never make yourself feel guilty about the process of taking care of yourself.

— s. mcnutt

You love the same way I do—all in, giving too much, loving too hard, and never looking out for yourself, because you put others first. I will never tell you to stop; however, I will tell you to be patient with dating because people like us have to pick the right partner. For us, the right partner will either build us or destroy us.

— s. mcnutt

I hope you get to be with
someone who is a home and
an adventure—a soul who both
calms you and drives you wild.

— s. mcnutt

Self-love is picking the right
partner, the right job, and the
right mindsets to live with.

— s. mcnutt

Words are extremely powerful.
Never use them to destroy; use
them to build.

— s. mcnutt

We always forget to thank
ourselves for the progress that
we have made on our journeys.
Imagine how we would feel
if we didn't focus on how far
we needed to go, but instead
we focused on how far we
have come.

— s. mcnutt

They say you're selfish for putting yourself first; however, self-preservation is a behavior that ensures an organism's survival. How are you selfish for trying to make sure that you survive?

— s. mcnutt

There is this little voice in our head that tells us to be quiet, to care about everyone else's needs, and to break our spirit, all in the name of helping another person. Who the hell is going to help us? Who is going to look out for us? Nobody will; it's up to you to put yourself first. It's up to you to tell that voice that you need to put yourself first for a while.

— s. mcnutt

It is sexy to me when you take
care of yourself. Love yourself so
I can love you too.

— s. mcnutt

I need time to myself—space to
grow my mind, to heal deeply, to
learn who I really am.

— s. mcnutt

Some people don't understand the importance of solitude. I don't always want to be stimulated. I don't always want noise. In fact, when I find my alone time, that's when I find myself. Alone time helps me put myself first. It helps me reset life.

— s. mcnutt

My personality confuses people. I enjoy being alone a lot, but I'm very social and outgoing.

My environment dictates how I behave. Sometimes I'm loud, sometimes I'm quiet. I read the energy and adjust. There are times when I want to turn up with others and then there are moments when I want to read a good book, or process thoughts, alone. I am an ambivert.

— s. mcnutt

I need to be alone from time to time. Never think this desire of mine is because of something you did or did not do. It's not personal; I am wired like this.

— s. mcnutt

I no longer have space for friends or family members or lovers who do not understand that I must be afforded time to myself.

I will communicate it, I will show it, and I will be consistent with my efforts to put care into myself.

I will love you more when you understand this about me. I will love you forever when you allow me to navigate my alone time.

— s. mcnutt

In the generation of cell phones and online profiles, I still crave genuine human connection. I love sharing positive energy and laughter with others more than I love online.

— s. mcnutt

I am in my zone when I am alone. The right people will easily bring me out of my zone because nothing compares to a genuine connection. Most people have the wrong energy, and they keep me in my zone since I no longer have time for ulterior motives and disingenuous actions.

— s. mcnutt

Be mindful, extremely selective,
and very intentional about the
people you allow into your life.
Not enough people are talking
about how life-altering this is.

— s. mcnutt

I don't want to be around
pettiness, passive-aggressiveness,
unnecessary anger, extreme
bitterness, or any person who
brings me a nonpeaceful
vibration.

— s. mcnutt

I don't want to beg for communication, for understanding. I am comfortable in my own world, alone in my own space. If you want me to connect with you, please bring a mature and peaceful vibe; otherwise I would rather be left alone.

— s. mcnutt

We crave consistency so much that it kills desire. Relationships need to have desire to last. To me, it is one of the most powerful elements. Spend time apart so you can miss each other, so you can crave connection from one another.

— s. mcnutt

Most people don't understand
how draining they are. If you
need time to yourself, take it.

— s. mcnutt

Don't allow people to make
you feel bad because you enjoy
alone time or time to yourself
to gather your energy.

There's nothing wrong with
keeping to yourself and minding
your own business.

— s. mcnutt

This culture makes it seem like you have to slave away at a career to be happy.

I don't agree . . .

There has to be balance between work, life, education, friendships, and relationships. If you do not find the healthy balance, it is possible that you will always suffer. You have limited energy and limited hours in a day, so work diligently toward what's important to you, and realize that if you don't know how to balance, something will always suffer.

— s. mcnutt

Environment is truly everything in life. You can't settle for just anything. Cultivate a space that lifts you and others up and not one that holds everyone down.

— s. mcnutt

Sometimes a good soul will stay with the wrong person for too long, and it turns them bad. You have permission to walk away if the situation is pulling the worst behaviors out of you. Nobody is going to save you. Save yourself.

— s. mcnutt

I want to cultivate environments that produce ideas, sunshine, and laughter for everyone I know. We have all felt the depths of darkness for too long.

— s. mcnutt

I have to create and sustain an environment that is healthy. It's not just about me. It's about the kids, my lover, and my family. We all deserve to live in consistently healthy spaces. I will do whatever I have to do to cultivate this space. I'm putting myself first because all these people need me to be at my best.

— s. mcnutt

Don't stay in a toxic
environment and expect
it to give you clean air. If
you want to breathe again,
you know what you need to do.

— s. mcnutt

You'll feel a million times
better when you leave that
toxic relationship that you
no longer deserve to be in.
If you haven't had the strength
to leave, just know, your future
self is begging you to put
yourself first right now.

— s. mcnutt

When it is time to go, be gone.
Stop convincing yourself to stay
in unwanted environments.

— s. mcnutt

Your own joy comes first.
Eliminate anything that
threatens your ability to
stay happy.

Jobs can go. Fake friends
go. Those bad habits and
terrible mindsets that slow
you down must go.

Take control of your life,
you only get one. You are
strong enough to do this.

— s. mcnutt

If the job is toxic, leave.
You can get money from
a career that doesn't ruin
your happiness and health.

— s. mcnutt

Some people come into your
life to teach you a lesson. Not
everyone is permanent.

— s. mcnutt

Sometimes everything hits you all at once. You lose a relationship, change jobs, and old friends go and new friends come. It's up one day and down the next. You have it all together on Monday, and by Thursday you don't have a clue. Life is one big wave, and all we can do is flow, grow, and adapt. Understand when it's time to let go.

— s. mcnutt

I am not for everyone, but
once you taste my energy,
you'll always be thirsty.

— s. mcnutt

You can learn something from
everyone but you also do not
have to. Some people have energy
that just doesn't combine well,
like oil and water.

— s. mcnutt

When your emotions get the best of you, pause, breathe, gather facts, and allow things to play out. Self-care is being patient versus blowing up.

— s. mcnutt

Emotional people make situations worse because they stop thinking. They respond with ego. Sit back, inhale deeply, and approach it methodically.

— s. mcnutt

Break up with the negative
self-talk, with telling yourself
what you cannot do, with self-
sabotage. Get angry about this,
and use the anger to power you.
You're worth more than what
you've allowed, and now it's time
to get serious about yourself.
You can do this. Save yourself.

— s. mcnutt

Self-love is putting yourself
in as many situations that
allow you to smile, to hug,
and to feel valued and wanted.

— s. mcnutt

EIGHT

OVERCOMING ANXIETY

The hardest thing a young boy will do in his life is go talk to the pretty girl in his class. He plays the scenario over in his head a million times. Dealing with rejection, failure, and the potential of what may happen can slow us all. Your eyes get large and your hands begin to sweat for a reason. Let's talk about how we can embrace and lean into anxiety.

Overthinking may ruin happiness and opportunity, and it can create unneeded anxiety. You're overthinking so much because you want to control the outcomes. The only things you can control are your effort and your attitude—that's it. Alternative: tell yourself you deserve it and then take the necessary actions so you can earn it.

— s. mcnutt

Overthinking is the biggest waste of human energy. Trust yourself, make a decision, and gain more experience. There is no such thing as perfect. You cannot think your way into perfection; just take action.

— s. mcnutt

A Letter on Anxiety

I used to deal with crippling anxiety, and here's what I did to get rid of it. I accepted that I used to try to control every detail about an environment. I would run if it felt challenging. And that's when I realized that the feeling of anxiety makes you feel like everything is challenging, but I knew my mind was stronger, and so I ran face-first into situations. It was scary at first, but the more I did it, the more comfortable I became. And then I realized that anxiety was all in my head, and it's been gone ever since that day.

With compassion,

Sylvester McNutt III

A lot of us are afraid to face ourselves, and that is why we run from growth, love, or opportunity. Instead, we run into anxiety.

— s. mcnutt

What would happen to your life if you stopped disliking that thing about yourself that someone else told you to dislike?

— s. mcnutt

Spend less time overthinking
and more time trusting your
intuition and setting boundaries.

— s. mcnutt

If your intuition tells you that
something is off, pause, don't
react emotionally right away, and
be patient as you fully observe
behavior and energy.

— s. mcnutt

If you want your relationship to be beautiful, you have to be comfortable with having uncomfortable and sometimes ugly conversations.

— s. mcnutt

When I had the most anxiety, it was because I wanted to control every outcome. I was not confident in myself and overthought every scenario 47 times. Once I broke up with the need to control the external, the anxiety went away.

— s. mcnutt

Mindfulness allows you to stay in the moment. Staying in the moment allows you to not stress or worry about the future. This practice eases and eliminates anxiety.

— s. mcnutt

Mindfulness is the ability to fill your mind with your full attention to the present moment. Mindfulness allows you to stay here, to erase anxiety, because anxiety is created via stress from a future event, outcome, or emotion.

— s. mcnutt

Never stress about money;
the stress only makes it worse
than it has to be.

— s. mcnutt

Make a written budget and
commit to it. Increase your
income and decrease your
expenses. Lastly, tell yourself
that you are worthy of financial
abundance, and then trust
the process.

— s. mcnutt

No matter how much you worry, complain, or stress out about something, the result will still be the same. Learn to live in a space of acceptance. It will free you.

— s. mcnutt

Your anxiety exists because you are uncertain about the outcome of certain events, and the truth is, nothing in life is certain—nothing.

— s. mcnutt

Some anxiety is based on
irrational fears. Ask yourself:
How real is this fear in
this moment?

— s. mcnutt

If you don't examine your fears,
they will control you for the rest
of your life. Sometimes, you have
to be brave and wild, and just say,
"Fuck it; I trust myself; let's see
what happens."

— s. mcnutt

I used to have a bad case of anxiety with certain situations and people. It went away for me when I realized every human has a level of anxiety that they experience. When I stopped judging myself and when I learned to trust my intuition, the anxiety went away and life became easier for me.

— s. mcnutt

Fear makes your anxiety spike, and that's why you have to change the dialogue in your head about what real fear is versus what you have created.

— s. mcnutt

If you get panic attacks caused by anxiety, remember this: breathe and pause. You will have thoughts, but try your best to have positive inner thoughts while breathing deeply.

— s. mcnutt

There is no value in allowing others' opinions to rule who you are or who you're going to be.

— s. mcnutt

One of the best ways to worry less and smile more is to remove the obsessive need to control outcomes or perceptions. *To be okay with what is.*

— s. mcnutt

If you struggle with anxiety, you have to applaud yourself every single time you step outside of your comfort zone.

— s. mcnutt

Don't worry or allow yourself
to stress about problems. They
come. You apply attention
and energy to them, and then
they go away.

— s. mcnutt

We are all guilty of obsessing
about the end point of the
journey, and the truth is, there
is no end point to any journey.
Everything is connected.
Everything matters, and this
is why you have to learn to
appreciate the moments, to be
totally immersed in the journey.

— s. mcnutt

Dear Human Dealing with Anxiety,

In some cases, your anxiety is normal. Anxiety itself is an experience that every person feels on some level.

It's okay and normal to experience anxiety, nervousness, angst, and worry throughout life. I've found the key to healing social anxiety, self-doubt, overthinking, and worry. They all went away when I did two things: First, I started controlling my breathing. Second, I started to control my inner dialogue about what I was experiencing.

If this doesn't help, please see a therapist and please do not have any shame about it. It's okay if you need help. It's okay if you want to talk to a professional about it, one who can help you declutter your experience.

With compassion,
Sylvester McNutt III

NINE

LIVING IN THE MOMENTS

A collection of words, thoughts, and poems that were inspired by the art of staying in the moment.

When was the last time you
turned the phone off, stayed away
from social media and the news,
and just sat with yourself?

— s. mcnutt

The practice of staying present
will heal you. Obsessing about
how the future will turn out
creates anxiety. Replaying broken
scenarios from the past causes
anger or sadness.

Stay here, in this moment.

— s. mcnutt

Just Handle It

The idea that you have to "figure out" your entire life by the time you're twenty-five makes me laugh. Life doesn't work that way. Stay self-aware, focus on growth, and just enjoy every moment.

— s. mcnutt

I am the type of person who needs to move forward more than I need to stay stuck in the past.

— s. mcnutt

I don't derive my sense of self from who I was in the past. I have grown. I am who I am today. I live in the present energy of who I am today.

— s. mcnutt

I have learned to live in a space
of gratitude—staying grateful for
what I have, learning from what
I have lost, and never breaking
my mind by wanting to be
where I am not.

— s. mcnutt

Stay in the Moment

We are the generation of
looking down at our cell phones
while we miss so much beautiful
life. When was the last time that
you truly felt the wind wrap
around your skin? When was the
last time that you really listened
to music? Not just heard but
really listened?

— s. mcnutt

When on a date, stay off your *phone* and stay plugged into the art of connecting.

— s. mcnutt

You always talk about your *mistakes*—stop. There are no mistakes. All we have are lessons and information about what has happened or is happening.

— s. mcnutt

We convince ourselves that
there is a right way and a wrong
way to live, and there's not.
There is only reality and fantasy.
There is only what is and what
we hope it to be. The more we
live in reality, the better off
we will be.

— s. mcnutt

Society has conditioned us to
believe that we need to always
live in the future, that we need to
always be planning and reaching
for something that we don't have.
Let's reject that. There is nothing
wrong with staying present and
remaining grateful for what we
have today.

— s. mcnutt

Work hard, but know when it's time to rest. Working all the time with no breaks, without recharging is silly. Self-care is about recovery too. Give yourself time off so you can reset.

— s. mcnutt

While society tries to convince us that the only way is to obsess about work and wanting more, I am a part of the crazy collective who will tell you to obsess about self-awareness, mental health, deep connections, love, and sustained happiness.

— s. mcnutt

Most people fail because they do not plan. They do not execute when they do plan, and they quit as soon as something gets hard. I plan to continue to plan, to follow through with massive action, and to persevere during tough times. This is the blueprint for success that I am following until I no longer breathe.

— s. mcnutt

When you spend so much time thinking about who you might be in the future, all you give yourself is anxiety and uncertainty. Stay in the moment and focus on today. Take time to create your future, but never obsess about the story lines of tomorrow.

— s. mcnutt

After you've been broken so much, you find this surreal inner strength—a strength that always allows you to put yourself back together.

— s. mcnutt

I dealt with abandonment issues when I was younger. I would beg the wrong people to stay, and I would fight to keep people who didn't want to be kept, all because I didn't want to be alone. I didn't want to face myself. After I healed, grew, and became comfortable with myself, I realized something so powerful: those who want to be around will, and those who do not will run for the hills. Now I build with who wants to stay, and I help them pack if they want to go.

— s. mcnutt

A Letter on Letting Them Go

Don't you dare break your back anymore carrying the weight of people who do not desire to be carried—people who want to run for the hills and escape you. If they want to live life without you, let them go. Let them be free. Make sure you always do your best with people while they're around you, but even your best won't be good enough for some people, and that's okay. When they want to run, don't feel like you need to internalize all the pain like everything is your fault and like there are a million things wrong with you. Never take it personally, because they have a choice, and if they want to go, they should be allowed to go.

— s. mcnutt

The Moment You Want
to Snap on Someone, Don't

Anger gets us. We feel pain that we know damn well we don't deserve to feel, and of course, we want revenge. We want them to feel what we are feeling.

Don't do it. Don't get even. Don't retaliate. Don't get petty. Adjust, change, adapt, and figure out a new plan moving forward.

Maybe it's time to cut ties—to put your foot down—or maybe you just need to show them that they cannot control your emotions with theirs. Don't snap. Keep a level head and walk away.

— s. mcnutt

We just saw a movie on Christmas Eve. While walking to our car, I overheard a conversation. A group of homeless men were laughing and teasing one another. The one on the ground looked up at the other and said, "I know you haven't eaten today. Please, just take my tacos. It's steak, bro. I know you love steak." With a tear in his eye and a smile on his face, the man accepted the tacos from the other man. It was at that moment that I realized I didn't deserve to complain or be ungrateful ever again in my life. This moment taught me that even when you have nothing, you still have everything.

— s. mcnutt

If It's Not Genuine,
Keep It Away

I retired from dealing with the fake version of people. I only want your authentic self, no matter how dark or deep it is. I don't expect perfection from myself or you, but I do expect real. I do expect honest. Is it genuine? If so, feed me more.

— s. mcnutt

A Letter to Myself on Anger

Oh, dear anger, it's so good to meet you again.

Sarcasm at its finest. You have become my best friend lately. When I was younger, I knew you every day. In fact, I was you; you were me. As they say, we were two peas in a pod. You helped me be violent because all I knew was violence. You helped me harm myself and others.

You helped me love to be reckless. I haven't hung out with you in so long. In fact, I made you a stranger for a while, but you've found your way back into my life. I stopped letting people get to me. I stopped caring about petty, irrelevant, irrational things. I became Zen, calm, untriggered. I proactively healed and managed my pain. I took care of business, so we never hung out.

Most people fear anxiety or public speaking or talking to girls. I know people who fear death and driving and alcoholism. My biggest fear is anger; my biggest fear is you manifesting your dirty talons in my heart again.

Anger turns me into the Hulk, into a madman, into a statistic. So now that I've been hanging out with you, you're starting to feel normal again.

You're starting to convince me that I should drink, which is a promise I made to myself. I promised myself I would never drink if you were around me.

Growing up with alcoholic parents is the easiest way to become an alcoholic. I mean, damn, my parents showed me that it was okay to lose your life in a bottle every night. They showed me it was okay to fall into the base of nothingness and blame Jack Daniels. I'm not sure who my father had a better relationship with: was it with my mother or was it with Jack? My mom cheated on my father every night with a six-pack of Miller Genuine Draft. They couldn't commit to each other, but they could commit to the sorrows at the bottom of the bottle, which then helped them commit to violence and unruliness.

This is why I don't drink when I am angry. Those people that they were are inside of me, locked deep down inside of me, and even though I've never been what I just decried, I also never want to become it. This is why I have an inconsistent relationship with alcohol. This is why I promised myself that I would never drink when I was angry. The second that I drink when I'm angry, that is the moment when I lose everything. That is when I transform into the raging beast. The mechanic who has no tools. The athlete who has no sport or team. The person who is lost in life.

With love,
Sylvester McNutt III

Dear Anger,

I'm going to pray, I'm going to meditate, and I'm going to take every action I can to let you die. You don't deserve to live inside my temple. You no longer have power—I do. So leave. Take my ego with you, and allow me to have the peace that I deserve.

— s. mcnutt

I am on the path to figuring out how to increase my income and decrease my expenses. I don't care to be broke, to be struggling, or to still be figuring things out forever. I broke up with the mindset of staying on the consistent struggle bus years ago. I need connections who care about financial wellness the same as physical fitness and spiritual understanding.

— s. mcnutt

An Open Letter to Trust Issues

Hello again.

So nice to see you. So nice to have you join my life again. I've come to realize that your existence is the death of all relationships. I've never seen a relationship recover from your presence. Does it happen? I'm sure it does somewhere, but never in my world. Never in the history of my life have I seen a relationship recover to be what it was once, and that's not a pessimistic view; it's just realistic. After trust has been broken, people always change into something else. In fact, sometimes the lack of trust helps the two people create trust. Amazing how that works.

Sometimes it helps people get more serious about each other, about why they're in the relationship, and about how they're going to treat each other. So you're right. No relationship is the same when trust issues creep in, but it also doesn't mean that it's over either.

With compassion,
Sylvester McNutt III

I don't like putting all my personal business on the Internet. It's not that I have things to hide. That's not it. I don't know you, Internet people, and I don't owe anyone on the Internet anything. I'd rather keep my real life in my real life and just know that the Internet life is what I want you to see.

— s. mcnutt

Simple: if worrying about your opinion gives me anxiety, then I mustn't worry about your opinion.

— s. mcnutt

Grow out of feeling like every step you take needs to be liked by others. On your path to be great, others may not understand the sacrifices that you'll have to make, but you still have to do them anyways.

— s. mcnutt

Needing approval from others will always make you scared, will always make you anxious, and will never allow you to trust yourself. Empower yourself. Be willing to take a chance on you, and if others dislike you, oh well.

— s. mcnutt

Always value your community. Nothing is more important than family, than laughing with lovers, than making memories that you might forget with people you'll always remember.

— s. mcnutt

Privacy is important. There isn't much you need to know about me. I reserve that space for a select group of people.

— s. mcnutt

10 Reasons Why You Should Not Care about Their Opinion

1. It has never paid any of your bills.
2. It will not be there when you are sick.
3. It does not give you orgasms.
4. It has never made me you a better person.
5. It is negative and egocentric.
6. It doesn't uplift, challenge, or encourage.
7. It came from them, not you.
8. It will not marry you or carry your casket.
9. It is not based on facts.
10. It does not determine your worth.

A Lot Can Happen in a Year

People die. You outgrow old friends and get tired of mundane jobs. New careers come. New friends find your soul. But no matter what, you grow, you lose your mind a little bit, and most importantly, you get a little wiser. Your circle gets smaller because you get stricter with your energy and time. If you're really lucky, you'll find love inside of yourself, inside of friends and family, and just maybe the universe will bless you with a lover who laughs at your lame jokes.

— s. mcnutt

TEN

KEEP LOVING

No matter what, we have to keep loving.

No matter what darkness
life brings me, I will choose
the light of love, for that light
shines the brightest.

— s. mcnutt

If being single causes you inner
stress, think about this: Who
told you that you're required
to be in a "relationship" to feel
love? Love isn't exclusive to
dating. We feel love with friends,
family, inside of ourselves; love is
everywhere, all the time.

— s. mcnutt

The art of loving yourself means you learn to appreciate and accept every little thing about who you are today. You stop judging yourself based on who you might be and you've made peace with who you once were.

— s. mcnutt

Learn who you are. Unlearn who they told you to be.

— s. mcnutt

There are too many people
who are at war with their
own brain. Forgive yourself
and end the war.

— s. mcnutt

You cannot win the
battle of life if you are
always at war with yourself.

Surrender and let go
of the position that you
need to fight yourself—
you don't.

— s. mcnutt

Everyone is allegedly busy;
however, people make time
for those they care about.
They make excuses for those
whom they do not.

— s. mcnutt

It doesn't take much to call and
say, "I didn't want anything. Just
want to say hello and hear your
voice." That type of treatment
goes a long way.

— s. mcnutt

I hope you cultivate the
friendships that give value
to you and them. Friends who
push each other to grow, who
call each other to laugh, who are
there for each other through the
ups and the downs. I hope you
find the friends who love to see
you smile, but they're there for
you when you need to cry.

— s. mcnutt

I want to be the kind of friend
you can count on no matter
what. I'll give you my last cup of
water, walk with you in a storm,
and swim across an ocean if it'll
make your life better.

— s. mcnutt

Your partner has to be your biggest fan and vice versa. They should celebrate your victories as if they were their own successes.

— s. mcnutt

You deserve to be with someone who doesn't make you feel crazy for being a complex human being.

— s. mcnutt

Sometimes our soul mate
is sitting right across from
us at the coffee shop, and
we never stop to say hello.
Open up more.

— s. mcnutt

I am here to love people, to
make others smile, to be
someone's strength when
they have lost their own.

— s. mcnutt

If you want your relationship to last, you have to learn to be quiet and listen to your partner's wants and needs.

— s. mcnutt

When you're loved by the wrong person, they take the simplest desires and make you feel crazy for wanting them. Never believe that you are crazy for wanting respect, communication, and some encouragement.

Those are the basics.

— s. mcnutt

Be the type of couple who
believes in supporting each
other's endeavors—a couple
who believes in encouraging
each other with positive action
and talk. Life is too short to
be with someone who is not
invested in you.

— s. mcnutt

Many people in this generation
quit way too soon. They want
full-time results but only put
in part-time efforts. When it
gets this tough, most people
quit, but you're not regular. You
keep fighting. You keep giving
it your all.

— s. mcnutt

I know it's hard for you, stuck in a generation that doesn't care about love and connection like you. You're a conversation starter. You're the type of person who digs deep.

You ask questions. Don't change that quality about you. We need more people who care about people.

— s. mcnutt

The pain bodies from the past
will always resurface if you
do not manage them today.
Sometimes the only way to create
something beautiful today is to
learn from the ugly thing that
destroyed you yesterday.

— s. mcnutt

Sometimes there will be people
in your life who will need you
more than you need them. When
it's your time, be there. Have
their back and do what is needed
so they can fly, but always know
when to pull back so they can
eventually spread their wings on
their own.

— s. mcnutt

Never fall in love with someone's skin, status, or money. Fall in love with their personality, with their humor, with their smile.

— s. mcnutt

Just because there is love there, that doesn't mean we have to give every little piece of ourselves so that others feel complete.

— s. mcnutt

Tough love is real love too.
Sometimes you have to say
no, and you can do that
compassionately, with grace.
Don't demean, put down, or
make people feel like they're less
than you because you have to say
no. Also, do not guilt yourself
into negative emotions.

— s. mcnutt

Grow a healthy relationship.
Talk about finances, wants,
needs, goals. Support and
encourage. Work through hard
days, and touch each other daily.

— s. mcnutt

Four Ways to Instantly Make Your Relationship Vibrate Higher

1. Tell them deeply and genuinely why you appreciate them.

2. Thank them for their efforts to better themselves.

3. Ask them to go for a walk instead of watching TV.

4. Simply ask them, "How can I love you better?"

In life, in careers, in personal growth, and in all types of connections, alignment is everything.

— s. mcnutt

Too many people fall victim to forcing a connection, a moment, or the energy between two people. When you have found the right person, the vibe flows.

— s. mcnutt

Fake "I Miss You" Texts

I do not want to receive "I miss you" texts from people who have chosen to leave my life. You don't deserve to pop back into my life or to play with my time or my emotions just because you are lonely.

You're not allowed to just check on me if there is no purpose. Every action in my life now needs a purpose, and playing small talk with someone from the past just isn't on my list anymore.

— s. mcnutt

No matter what, never place blame or fault. Use your energy to grow, to love yourself harder, and to raise your vibration.

— s. mcnutt

Don't wait for a perfect situation. Find someone who understands loyalty like you. A person who doesn't give up during the hard times. That's as close to perfect as you'll ever find.

— s. mcnutt

Currently, the only thing I care about is spending valuable time with a few good people. I don't need quantity because for my spirit, it's all about quality.

— s. mcnutt

Love me. Bring the best out of
me. Challenge me to grow. If not,
leave me where you found me.

— s. mcnutt

I'm experienced in both
love and pain. All I want is to
decrease the pain from the
past and love hard in my
near future.

— s. mcnutt

I never want you to feel
incomplete as my lover.
Teach me how to hold you,
how to make you smile,
and how to comfort you
when you cry.

— s. mcnutt

Be the person I can cry with
when I'm sad or happy. Be the
person who will allow me to
open up and be vulnerable
without fear. Be there for me
when I can't be there for myself,
and I promise to return it all.

— s. mcnutt

If we are apart, be willing to listen to the same song as me at the same time. Be willing to text me a million things about your day. Be willing to sit on FaceTime with me in your underwear, even if we aren't speaking. Just be willing.

— s. mcnutt

Primarily I know
I will die. Before that
day comes, I simply
want to love and be loved.
Everything else is secondary.

— s. mcnutt

All you do is give and give,
and I hope you know everyone
in your life is not able to thank
you. However, I thank you. I
appreciate you. I see how hard
you work on yourself, and I see
how hard you smile when you
make other people happy. On
behalf of everyone who is in your
life, including me,

Thank you.

— s. mcnutt

ELEVEN

HEALING

These final reminders are short poems, thoughts, and ideas rooted in healing—words you can always refer to when you don't have much time, but you crave some healing words.

I hope you approach healing as a process and not as a button. I hope you know that no matter how well you think you're doing, no matter how much greatness you've manifested, healing is always a part of any growing process.

Never feel like you are too good or above self-care, self-love, or resetting your life.

Healing requires
patience; healing is a
process, not a light switch.

— s. mcnutt

Drink more water. Water
heals you, and if you don't
like the taste, add lemon,
cucumber, mint, or lime.

— s. mcnutt

If I try and fail, it's okay. I want
to live fully and die empty.

— s. mcnutt

You have to fail in order to
succeed. It's a part of the process
of fulfilling your dreams.

— s. mcnutt

Don't drink alcohol just because of peer pressure or society. If you want tea, water, or juice, drink that and don't conform to what everyone else is doing.

— s. mcnutt

I challenge you to drink less alcohol and drink more tea.

— s. mcnutt

I challenge you to care about your health more and your social status less.

— s. mcnutt

12 HEALING CHALLENGES

1. No alcohol for 90 days.

2. No complaining for seven days.

3. Journal every night this month.

4. Respect your boundaries all day.

5. Say yes all day to embrace the present.

6. Journal every day for the next 30 days.

7. Be more empathic in conversations today.

8. Praise your partner every time you critique.

9. Say no all day to embrace your boundaries.

10. Go for a 30 minute walk every morning this month.

11. Speak in a compassionate tone when you are frustrated.

12. Take 30–60 minutes to make an intentional and nourishing meal.

Vibrate Higher

Alcohol lowers your inhibitions, which is your ability to rationalize a good decision from a bad one. Raise your vibration and drink less. Never drink past your limit, or just avoid the entire scene.

— s. mcnutt

Don't use alcohol to cope with pain. Instead, make some tea, and journal. Go talk to someone. Go to the gym. Do not turn to alcohol when you are mad, sad, or in pain. It will ruin you.

— s. mcnutt

When you wake up, avoid the cell phone. Get some water, stretch, spend time alone. Do what you have to do to create the proper energy needed to seize the day.

— s. mcnutt

Some of your friends and family members are low vibrational. Don't commit to entertaining them due to blind loyalty. Sometimes you have to just go away and save yourself.

— s. mcnutt

Hanging out with the unlucky,
the unhappy, the angry, and the
unruly will always make you
vibrate lower.

— s. mcnutt

Vibrate higher by
distancing yourself
from those friendships
that offer consistent
struggle and pain.

— s. mcnutt

Sometimes your purpose is
to be the best teammate and
costar. Help them. Grow with
them. Take whatever role you
must in order for the team to
get a victory.

— s. mcnutt

The best kind of teammates pick
each other up when one falls,
they push each other to be great,
and they have each other's back
until it's all over.

— s. mcnutt

Stop chasing communication
from adults who claim to be
your friends but never call or text
back. We are all busy, but even
still, busy is no longer an excuse.

— s. mcnutt

Fact: people make time for
people they care about.

— s. mcnutt

Take time out of your night
to stretch, to read, to heal.

— s. mcnutt

The problem is that most people
do not have time management
skills. Everyone has time—that
can no longer be the excuse.

— s. mcnutt

If I send you a song, it is because
the music made me think about
you, or even deeper, it's helping
me explain who I am to you in a
way that I cannot.

— s. mcnutt

Vibrate higher by paying
attention to the energy that
the music you listen to carries.
Sometimes it builds, and other
times it destroys.

— s. mcnutt

Corporate America, in some
cases, creates toxic environments
that will get you sick.
Sometimes you must leave these
places to heal.

— s. mcnutt

You have sick days and planned
days off for a reason. Use them
to focus on healing, on recovery,
and on the fun things that you
care about.

— s. mcnutt

Don't stay in a job environment
if it kills your joy, your identity,
and your happiness. *Find
your purpose.*

— s. mcnutt

You can get money a lot of ways
and from many different sources.
Don't stay stuck in a place just
because of money. If it hurts, if
it drains, if it causes depression,
there are other routes.

— s. mcnutt

When I get sick, I go away
from the world. I don't work;
I don't school; I go back to the
basics and focus on healing.
Everyone deserves the best of me,
including me, so excuse me while
I take time to heal.

— s. mcnutt

Employers think calling out
means you're sick with the cold
or flu, but that's only physical.
Mental health is important too,
and if my mind is not right, I will
not suffer and fake happiness on
that day. I will call out so I can
heal and come back better.

— s. mcnutt

Going to a job every day that I didn't love made me sick. I did what I had to do for as long as I had to do it, and then one day I woke up. I saw that it's better to do something you like, even if that means less money, than stay at a job you hate for more money.

— s. mcnutt

Pay more attention to fun, to hobbies, to rest, to things that spark you. School and work will always be calling you, so see what else life has to offer.

— s. mcnutt

Put the cell phone down more.
Doing this allows you to see
people's lies on your timeline
less often.

— s. mcnutt

A lot of people lie on social
media about who they are
because they have no idea who
they might be. Don't be a lot
of people.

You're not perfect, you're not
always right, and there is no
reason to pretend otherwise.

— s. mcnutt

Never create a perfect image of
yourself. It will make you sick
when you want to be imperfect
or real. Show your scars and your
flaws, and most importantly,
show that you embrace all of you.

— s. mcnutt

I don't show all of my personal
life on social media, for two
reasons: I like important and
special moments to stay private,
and none of you will be here
to help me build my life if
everything falls apart. Stop
acting like I owe you anything.

— s. mcnutt

You can instantly heal your life by stopping the process of putting all your business on social media. Move in private, let people guess, and allow your real friends to know the truth.

— s. mcnutt

Healing is getting rid of people or behaviors that have caused you to get sick.

— s. mcnutt

Healing is a formula.
Add what heals.
Subtract what hurts.
Learn from what goes.
Cherish what stays.

— s. mcnutt

Be patient while you shed old
skin and while new layers grow.

— s. mcnutt

Dear Society,

Fuck you for laughing at people
who need to cry aloud. We will
no longer suffer in silence.

— s. mcnutt

I have no shame in saying
I don't know. I have no shame
in asking for help after I have
failed. I have no problem
asking for more explanation.
I want to learn.

— s. mcnutt

Never be afraid to seek help
from a counselor, teacher,
health professional, friend, or
even a stranger. Don't hold
everything in.

— s. mcnutt

I hope my kids feel like I
am a beacon of support and
encouragement.

— s. mcnutt

I do not see the value in
spanking, hitting, or beating
children. A true master of
communication can connect
with a child. Many adults are
mad at their children because the
child mimics behavior that he or
she saw from the parents. How
can we beat someone who came
from us for acting like us?

— s. mcnutt

You can discipline children
without hitting them, without
screaming at them like you
hate them.

— s. mcnutt

We will make many mistakes as parents, but we should all have one goal: create an experience for our children that they do not have to heal from.

— s. mcnutt

Become fully aware of your inner dialogue. The key to true healing occurs in between those conversations you have with yourself.

— s. mcnutt

Becoming truly conscious of your thoughts doesn't mean that you're never negative or down. It means you identify it quickly. It means you acknowledge the low vibrational energy, work through your feelings, and move forward.

— s. mcnutt

To truly heal your life, make meditation a part of your daily routine. Practice silence—not speaking or obsessively thinking. Remain in a state of being and allow everything to flow.

— s. mcnutt

If you have trouble clearing your mind, that means you need to practice a session of mindfulness today. Pause your brain. Stop obsessing about thoughts, things you need to do, assignments, or deadlines. Sit still and breathe deeply with the intention of truly becoming one with your breath.

— s. mcnutt

If there is one thing that you can do right now to add more healing to your life, what would you guess it might be? *No, stalking your ex's social media is not the answer.* It's called meditation—breathing deeply with the intent of becoming one with the moment.

— s. mcnutt

Have you ever disliked or loved someone as soon as you met them? *Of course you have.* You are proof that vibrational energies are real and the energy we carry daily matters.

— s. mcnutt

The drama queen or king you know always says that they don't want drama, but they unconsciously keep triggering dramatic situations because that is the vibrational energy they are giving out. The universe is only matching what is already inside of them.

— s. mcnutt

Healing from the pain is not easy, you're right, *but it is possible to heal*. And that hope is all I need to know to keep smiling, to keep laughing, and to keep telling myself that everything is going to be okay.

— s. mcnutt

This was a tough pill to swallow, but once I did, I healed. I grew. I vibrated higher. Your success or your failure is 100 percent on you, on your effort, on your mindset, on your behaviors.

— s. mcnutt

Gratitude allows you to vibrate higher. It allows you to keep what you have. It allows you to water the plants that have already grown from your majestic garden.

— s. mcnutt

Don't obsess about what
you don't have. Look at what
you've lost. Learn from it, and
remain forever grateful for what
you do have.

— s. mcnutt

In some cases, wanting more
is a disease. Heal yourself by
cultivating a consistent space
of gratefulness.

— s. mcnutt

Investments

Keep it simple: stop
buying things
that do not enhance your life.

— s. mcnutt

The mission is to practice
investing: invest financially, save
money, increase your income,
invest in your health and well-
being, save energy, and increase
your happiness.

— s. mcnutt

Breaking Cell Phone Addiction

I took notifications off, all
e-mail, all games and useless
apps, all social media apps,
and anything that constantly
goes off. I keep sounds off
and brightness down. This all
helped me.

— s. mcnutt

Don't forget to unplug from the
cell phone, from social media,
from television, from other
people's opinions. There is a lot
of value in reconnecting with
your inner world.

— s. mcnutt

The cell phone is the most
powerful and the most
dangerous tool of our generation.
Use it wisely; do not use it
aimlessly.

— s. mcnutt

You will heal your sleep schedule
if you stay off your cell phone
and computer at least 30 to 40
minutes before it's time to rest.

— s. mcnutt

You can heal your peace of mind
by turning notifications off on
your cell phone. Keeping them
on always pulls your attention
away from the present moment.

— s. mcnutt

Heal your brain from the addiction that society has given us. Be intentional about going hours upon hours without checking your cell phone.

— s. mcnutt

Sometimes you need to leave your cell phone at home on purpose. Go to school, work, or to the gym with the intention to be fully alert, completely immersed in the present moment.

— s. mcnutt

We are at a point in society where people will say that they *need* their phones. This is a false claim. You need air, water, sleep, love, and belonging—human connection. If you go a few hours without your phone, you will survive.

— s. mcnutt

I care deeply about human connection. I desire to cultivate and sustain stimulating conversation, intriguing interaction, and new experiences.

— s. mcnutt

When people talk to you, put your phone down and look them in the eye. Give feedback and engage in conversation. The time line and text messages will always be there.

— s. mcnutt

More people need to understand
that scrolling your phone
aimlessly when other humans
are trying to communicate is
nonverbal feedback that tells
them you're uninterested in
connecting with them.

— s. mcnutt

In the generation of *phone in my
hand*, I respect anyone who can
put it away and engage, people
who crave human connection
like I do.

— s. mcnutt

I challenge you to set aside
time each day to cultivate "cell
phone–free time." Time to
stretch, to read, to write, to draw,
to paint, to lift, to swim, to go
for a hike, to do anything other
than scrolling vibes.

— s. mcnutt

If it brings you constant
stress and discomfort, please
understand this: it is trying to
teach you something.

— s. mcnutt

Fall in love with taking care of yourself. Fall in love with the path of deep healing. Fall in love with becoming the best version of yourself but with patience, with compassion, and respect for your own journey.

— s. mcnutt

Promise yourself that after you read this you will break up with self-sabotage, you will stop talking down to yourself, and you will try your hardest to breathe and let some things go.

— s. mcnutt

You have survived the worst already; you are still here winning, and fighting. Just keep loving, be patient with healing, and lead with love and joy.

— s. mcnutt

Be less serious and have more fun. Think more about the moment and less about the future or past. The main thing you need more of in your life, is more happiness, and you deserve it too.

— s. mcnutt

Trust the vibes you get; energy doesn't lie.

— s. mcnutt

Energy is everything and it is everywhere. It's in the food you eat, the music you listen to, and the people you surround yourself with. Always pay attention to energy.

— s. mcnutt

THANK YOU FOR READING

Care Package: Harnessing the Power of Self-Compassion to Heal & Thrive

I dedicate this to us. We have been through a lot, but we are recovering, we are loving, and we are fighting for us and those around us. Our main goal should be to focus on getting rid of the pain, and we know it's not *easy*, but it is possible. I hope *Care Package* showed you and brought you words that make you believe that. Healing from the pain is not easy, you're right, but it is possible to heal. And that hope is all I need to know to keep smiling, to keep laughing, and to keep telling myself that everything is going to be okay. I am thankful that you allowed *Care Package* to assist you on this journey. Please take the time to reflect, to write, to travel, to do whatever is going to allow you to marinate with your own energy. Take a day off of work or school to sit in nature if it will allow you to figure things out. Stay inspired and stay motivated. Lastly,

I need your help too. Please go leave a positive review for the *Care Package* book on Amazon.com and any other site that you visit. Reviews help me, the self-published author, find new readers. Your review could save someone's life, so please, do it as soon as possible. I love you all so much. I love you because you put yourself first today—thank you.

With compassion,
Sylvester McNutt III

ENDNOTES

1. Eckhart Tolle, *The Power of Now* (Vancouver: Namaste Publishing, 2004).
2. Melody Beattie, *Codependent No More* (Center City, MN: Hazelden Foundation, 1986).

ABOUT THE
AUTHOR

Sylvester McNutt III is a best-selling author, podcaster, public speaker, course creator, and father. Sylvester teaches people how to transform their mindsets through self-awareness and healing practices. As a retired arena football player and survivor of traumatic experiences, Sylvester has used storytelling to teach people how to introspect, gain confidence, and sustain self-love. Sylvester's core belief is that healing is the key to success & self-awareness unlocks freedom. Sylvester's passions are writing, lifting, traveling, yoga, and exploring the human existence.

www.sylvestermcnutt.net

Hay House Titles of Related Interest

YOU CAN HEAL YOUR LIFE, the movie,
starring Louise Hay & Friends
(available as an online streaming video)
www.hayhouse.com/louise-movie

THE SHIFT, the movie,
starring Dr. Wayne W. Dyer
(available as an online streaming video)
www.hayhouse.com/the-shift-movie

*GOOD VIBES, GOOD LIFE: How Self-Love is the Key
to Unlocking Your Greatness,* by Vex King

*THE HIGH 5 HABIT: Take Control of Your Life
with One Simple Habit,* by Mel Robbins

*HOW TO BE LOVE(D): Simple Truths for Going Easier
on Yourself, Embracing Imperfection &
Loving Your Way to a Better Life,* by Humble the Poet

*THAT SUCKED. NOW WHAT?: How to Embrace the Joy
in Chaos and Find Magic in the Mess,* by Neeta Bhushan

*YOU'RE GOING TO BE OKAY: 16 Lessons on
Healing after Trauma,* by Madeline Popelka

All of the above are available at www.hayhouse.co.uk.